D0359855

STYLE GUIDE

OTHER ECONOMIST BOOKS

Guide to Analysing Companies
Guide to Business Modelling
Guide to Economic Indicators
Guide to the European Union
Guide to Financial Markets
Guide to Management Ideas
Numbers Guide

Business Ethics
China's Stockmarket
Economics
E-Commerce
E-Trends
Globalisation
Measuring Business Performance
Successful Innovation
Successful Mergers
Wall Street

Dictionary of Business
Dictionary of Economics
International Dictionary of Finance

Essential Director
Essential Finance
Essential Internet
Essential Investment

Pocket Asia
Pocket Europe in Figures
Pocket World in Figures

The Economist

STYLE GUIDE

THE ECONOMIST IN ASSOCIATION WITH
PROFILE BOOKS LTD

Published by Profile Books Ltd,
58A Hatton Garden, London EC1N 8LX
www.profilebooks.co.uk

Drawings by Rufus Segar

Typeset in EcoType by MacGuru Ltd
info@macguru.org.uk
Printed in Great Britain by St Edmundsbury Press

A CIP catalogue record for this book is available from the British Library

ISBN 1 86197 535 X

Contents

Preface vi

Introduction 1

A Note on Editing 4

Part I The Essence of Style 5

Part II American and British English 81

Part III Fact Checker and Glossary 97

Index 161

Preface

EVERY newspaper has its own style book, a set of rules telling journalists whether to write e-mail or email, Gadaffi or Qaddafi, judgement or judgment. *The Economist*'s style book does this and a bit more. It also warns writers of some common mistakes and encourages them to write with clarity and simplicity.

To make the style guide of wider general interest, additional material has been added, drawing on the series of reference books published under The Economist Books imprint. All the prescriptive judgments in this style guide, however, are directly derived from those used each week in writing and editing *The Economist*.

Throughout the text, bold type is used to indicate examples. Words in SMALL CAPITALS indicate a separate but relevant entry (except in the paragraphs headed ABBREVIATIONS, where the use of small capitals is discussed).

This new, updated and revised edition of "The Economist Style Guide" is in three sections. The first is based on the style book used by those who edit *The Economist*; it is largely the work of John Grimond, who has over the years been Britain, American and foreign editor. The second, on American and British English, describes some of the main differences between the two great English-speaking areas, in spelling, grammar and usage. The third part gathers together in one place lots of useful reference material.

Introduction

On only two scores can *The Economist* hope to outdo its rivals consistently. One is the quality of its analysis; the other is the quality of its writing. The aim of this style guide is to give general advice on writing, to point out some common errors and to set some arbitrary rules.

The first requirement of *The Economist* is that it should be readily understandable. Clarity of writing usually follows clarity of thought. So think what you want to say, then say it as simply as possible. Keep in mind George Orwell's six elementary rules ("Politics and the English Language", 1946):

1. Never use a METAPHOR, simile or other figure of speech which you are used to seeing in print.
2. Never use a long word where a SHORT WORD will do.
3. If it is possible to cut out a word, always cut it out.
4. Never use the passive where you can use the ACTIVE.
5. Never use a FOREIGN PHRASE, a scientific word or a JARGON word if you can think of an everyday English equivalent.
6. Break any of these rules sooner than say anything outright barbarous.

Readers are primarily interested in what you have to say. By the way in which you say it you may encourage them either to read on or to stop reading. If you want them to read on:

1. Do not be stuffy. "To write a genuine, familiar or truly English style", said Hazlitt, "is to write as anyone would speak in common conversation who had a thorough command or choice of words or who could discourse with ease, force and perspicuity setting aside all pedantic and oratorical flourishes."

Use the language of everyday speech, not that of spokesmen, lawyers or bureaucrats (so prefer **let** to **permit**, **people** to **persons**, **buy** to **purchase**, **colleague** to **peer**, **way out** to **exit**, **present** to **gift**, **rich** to **wealthy**, **break** to **violate**). Enron's **document-management policy** simply meant **shredding**. It is sometimes useful to talk of **human-rights abuses** but often the sentence can be rephrased more pithily and more accurately. **The army is accused of committing numerous human-rights abuses** probably means **The army is accused of torture and murder**.

Avoid, where possible, euphemisms and circumlocutions promoted by interest-groups. The **hearing-impaired** are simply **deaf. Female teenagers** are **girls**, not **women**. The **underprivileged** may be **disadvantaged**, but are more likely just **poor. Decommissioning** weapons means **disarming.**

And **man** sometimes includes **woman**, just as **he** sometimes makes do for **she** as well (see pages 33, 67). So long as you are not insensitive in other ways, few women will be offended if you do not use **or she** after every he.

> He or she which hath no stomach to this fight,
> Let him or her depart; his or her passport shall be made,
> And crowns for convoy put into his or her purse:
> We would not die in that person's company
> That fears his or her fellowship to die with us.

2. Do not be hectoring or arrogant. Those who disagree with you are not necessarily **stupid** or **insane**. Nobody needs to be described as silly: let your analysis prove that he is. When you express opinions, do not simply make assertions. The aim is not just to tell readers what you think, but to persuade them; if you use arguments, reasoning and evidence, you may succeed. Go easy on the oughts and shoulds.

3. Do not be too pleased with yourself. Don't boast of your own cleverness by telling readers that you correctly predicted something or that you have a scoop. You are more likely to bore or irritate them than to impress them. So keep references to *The Economist* to a minimum, particularly those of the we-told-you-so variety. References to "this correspondent" or "your correspondent" are always self-conscious and often self-congratulatory.

4. Do not be too chatty. **Surprise, surprise** is more irritating than informative. So is **Ho, ho**, etc.

5. Do not be too didactic. If too many sentences begin **Compare, Consider, Expect, Imagine, Look at, Note, Prepare for, Remember** or **Take**, readers will think they are reading a textbook (or, indeed, a style book).

6. Do not be sloppy in the construction of your sentences and paragraphs. Do not use a participle unless you make it clear what it applies to. A recent issue of *The Economist* contained the following:
When closed at night, the fear is that this would shut off rather

than open up part of the city centre.
Unlike Canary Wharf, the public will be able to go to the top to look out over the city.
Only a couple of months ago, after an unbroken string of successes in state and local elections, pollsters said ...

Don't overdo the use of **don't, isn't, can't, won't**, etc.

Use the subjunctive properly. If you are posing a hypothesis contrary to fact, you must use the subjunctive. Thus, **If Hitler were alive today, he could tell us whether he kept a diary**. If the hypothesis may or may not be true, you do not use the subjunctive: **If this diary is not Hitler's, we shall be glad we did not publish it**. If you have **would** in the main clause, you must use the subjunctive in the if clause. **If you were to disregard this rule, you would make a fool of yourself.**

In general, be concise. Try to be economical in your account or argument ("The best way to be boring is to leave nothing out" – Voltaire). Similarly, try to be economical with words. You might try Sydney Smith's advice: "As a general rule, run your pen through every other word you have written; you have no idea what vigour it will give to your style."

Do your best to be lucid. Simple sentences help. Keep complicated constructions and gimmicks to a minimum, if necessary by remembering the *New Yorker*'s comment: "Backward ran sentences until reeled the mind." Mark Twain described how a good writer treats sentences: "At times he may indulge himself with a long one, but he will make sure there are no folds in it, no vaguenesses, no parenthetical interruptions of its view as a whole; when he has done with it, it won't be a sea-serpent with half of its arches under the water; it will be a torch-light procession."

Long paragraphs, just like long sentences, can confuse the reader. "The paragraph," according to Fowler, "is essentially a unit of thought, not of length; it must be homogeneous in subject matter and sequential in treatment." Paragraphs of one sentence should be used only occasionally.

Clear thinking is the key to clear writing. "A scrupulous writer", observed Orwell, "in every sentence that he writes will ask himself at least four questions, thus: What am I trying to say? What words will express it? What image or idiom will make it clearer? Is this image fresh enough to have an effect? And he will probably ask himself two more: Could I put it more shortly? Have I said anything that is avoidably ugly?"

Scrupulous writers will also notice that their copy is edited only lightly and is likely to be used. It may even be read.

A note on editing

Editing has always made a large contribution to *The Economist*'s excellence. It should continue to do so. But editing on a screen is beguilingly simple. It is quite easy to rewrite an article without realising that one has done much to it at all: the cursor leaves no trace of crossings-out, handwritten insertions, rearranged sentences or reordered paragraphs. The temptation is to continue to make changes until something emerges which the editor himself might have written. One benefit of this is a tightly edited newspaper. One cost is a certain sameness. The risk is that the newspaper will turn into a collection of 70 or 80 articles which read as though they have been written by no more than half a dozen hands. *The Economist* has a single editorial outlook, and it is anonymous. But it is the work of many people, both in London and abroad, as its datelines testify. If the prose of our Tokyo correspondent is indistinguishable from the prose of our Nairobi correspondent, readers will feel they are being robbed of variety. They may also wonder whether these two people really exist, or whether the entire newspaper is not written in London. The moral for editors is that they should respect good writing. That is mainly what this style guide is designed to promote. It is not intended to impose a single style on all *The Economist*'s journalists. A writer's style, after all, should reflect his mind and personality. So long as they are compatible with *The Economist*'s, and so long as the prose is good, editors should exercise suitable self-restraint. Remember that your copy, too, will be edited. And even if you think you are not guilty, bear in mind this comment from John Gross:

> Most writers I know have tales to tell of being mangled by editors and mauled by fact-checkers, and naturally it is the flagrant instances they choose to single out – absurdities, outright distortions of meaning, glaring errors. But most of the damage done is a good deal less spectacular. It consists of small changes (usually too boring to describe to anyone else) that flatten a writer's style, slow down his argument, neutralise his irony; that ruin the rhythm of a sentence or the balance of a paragraph; that deaden the tone that makes the music. I sometimes think of the process as one of "desophistication".

John Grimond

PART I

THE ESSENCE OF STYLE

A

ABBREVIATIONS. Unless an abbreviation or acronym is so familiar that it is used more often than the full form (eg, **BBC**, **CIA**, **FBI**, **HIV**, **IMF**, **NATO**, **OECD**), or unless the full form would provide little illumination (eg, **AWACS**, **DNA**), write the words in full on first appearance: thus **Trades Union Congress** (not **TUC**). After the first mention, try not to repeat the abbreviation too often; so write **the agency** rather than **the IAEA**, **the Union** rather than **the EU**, the **Fund** rather than **the IMF**, to avoid spattering the page with capital letters. There is no need to give the initials of an organisation if it is not referred to again.

If an abbreviation can be pronounced (eg, **ETA**, **NATO**, **UNESCO**), it does not generally require the definite article. Other organisations, except companies, should usually be preceded by **the** (**the BBC**, **the ECB**, **the NHS** and **the UNCHR**).

Remember that the **FAO** is the **Food and Agriculture Organisation**, the **FDA** is the **Food and Drug Administration**, **IDA** is the **International Development Association**, the **MFA** is the **Multi-Fibre Arrangement**, **NAFTA** is the **North American Free-Trade Agreement** and the **PLO** is the **Palestine Liberation Organisation**.

Abbreviations that can be pronounced and are composed of bits of words rather than just initials should be spelled out in upper and lower case: **Cocom**, **Frelimo**, **Kfor**, **Legco**, **Mercosur**, **Nepad**, **Renamo**, **Unicef**, **Unison**, **Unprofor**. (See also INITIALS.) But write **AIDS**, **UNITA**.

In text, abbreviations, whether they can be pronounced as words or not (**GNP**, **GDP**, **FOB**, **CIF**, **T-shirts**, **X-rays**), should be set in small capitals, with no points, unless they are currencies like **SKr** or **HK$**, elements like **H** and **O** or degrees of temperature like **°F** and **°C**. Brackets, apostrophes (see PUNCTUATION) and all other typographical furniture accompanying small capitals are generally set in ordinary roman, with a lower-case s (also roman) for plurals and genitives. Thus **IOUs**, **MPs'** salaries, **SDRs**, etc.

But ampersands are set as small capitals, as are numerals and any hyphens attaching them to a small capital. Thus **R&D**, **A23**, **M1**, **F-16**, etc. See also AMPERSANDS.

Abbreviations that include upper-case and lower-case letters must be set in a mixture of small capitals and lower case: **BAe, BPhil, PhDs.**

Always spell out **page, pages, hectares, miles.** But **kilograms** (not **kilogrammes**) and **kilometres** can be shortened to **kg** (or **kilos**) and **km.**

Do not use small caps for roman numerals.

Use lower case for **kg, km, lb** (never **lbs**), **kph, mph** and other MEASURES, and for **ie, eg,** which should both be followed by commas. When used with figures, these lower-case abbreviations should follow immediately, with no space (**11.30am, 15kg, 35mm, 100mph**), as should **AD** and **BC** (**AD76, 55BC**), although they are set in small capitals. Two abbreviations together, however, must be separated: **60m b/d.**

Most scientific units, except those of temperature, that are named after individuals should be set in small capitals, though any attachments denoting multiples go in lower case. Thus a **watt** is **W,** whereas **kilowatt, milliwatt** and **megawatt,** meaning **1,000 watts, one-thousandth of a watt** and **1m watts,** are abbreviated to **kW, MW** and **mW.**

The elements do not take small capitals. **Lead** is **Pb, carbon dioxide** is **CO_2, methane** is **CH_4. Chlorofluorocarbons** are, however, **CFCs,** and the oxides of nitrogen are generally **NOX.** Different isotopes of the same element are distinguished by raised prefixes: **carbon-14** is **^{14}C, helium-3** is **^{3}He.**

Most upper case abbreviations take upper case initial letters when written in full (eg, the **LSO** is the **London Symphony Orchestra**), but there are exceptions: **CAP** but **common agricultural policy, EMU** but **economic and monetary union, GDP** but **gross domestic product, PSBR** but **public-sector borrowing requirement, VLSI** but **very large-scale integration.**

Do not use **Prof, Sen, Gen, Col,** etc. But **Lieut-Colonel** and **Lieut-Commander** are permissible. So is **Rev,** but it must be preceded by **the** and followed by a Christian name or initial: **the Rev Jesse Jackson** (thereafter **Mr Jackson**). Always use **chief executive** or **boss** rather than **CEO.**

Remember, too, that the v of **HIV** stands for virus, so do not write **HIV virus.**

Members of Parliament are **MPs**; of the **Scottish Parliament, MSPs**; and of the **European Parliament, MEPs** (not **Euro-MPs**).

Spell out in full (and lower case) **junior** and **senior** after a name: **George Bush junior, George Bush senior.**

-ABLE, -EABLE, -IBLE. The following lists are not comprehensive.

-able

debatable	indictable	tradable
dispensable	indispensable	unmistakable
disputable	indistinguishable	unshakable
forgivable	lovable	unusable
imaginable	movable	usable
implacable	salable (but prefer sellable)	
indescribable		

-eable

bridgeable	rateable	unenforceable
knowledgeable	serviceable	unpronounceable
likeable	sizeable	
manageable	traceable	

-ible

accessible	inadmissible	irresistible
convertible	indestructible	permissible
digestible	investible	submersible

ACCENTS. On words now accepted as English, use accents only when they make a crucial difference to pronunciation: **cliché**, **soupçon**, **façade**, **café**, **communiqué**, **exposé**, **attaché** (but **chateau**, **decor**, **elite**, **feted**, **naive**). If you use one accent (except the tilde), use all: **émigré**, **mêlée**, **protégé**, **résumé**. See also ACCENTS, page 101.

Put the accents and cedillas on French names and words, umlauts on German ones, accents and tildes on Spanish ones, and accents, cedillas and tildes on Portuguese ones: **Françoise de Panafieu**, **Wolfgang Schäuble**, **Federico Peña**.

Leave the accents off names in other foreign languages. Any foreign word in italics should, however, be given its proper accents.

ACRONYM: this is a word, like **radar** or **NATO**, not a set of initials, like the **BBC** or the **IMF**.

ACTIVE, NOT PASSIVE. Be direct. **A hit B** describes the event more concisely than **B was hit by A**.

ADVERBS. Put adverbs where you would put them in normal speech, which is usually after the verb. But see also AMERICANISMS and PART II.

AFFECT, the verb, means to have an influence on, as in **The novel affected his attitude to immigrants**. See also EFFECT.

AFFINITY is by definition mutual. It can exist **between** or **with** things, but not **to** or **for** them.

AGGRAVATE means **make worse**, not **irritate** or **annoy**.

AGGRESSION is an unattractive quality, so do not call a **keen** salesman an aggressive one (unless his foot is in the door – or beyond).

AGONY COLUMN: when Sherlock Holmes perused this, it was a **personal column**, not letters to an **agony aunt**.

AGREE: things are agreed **on, to** or **about**, not just agreed.

AIRCRAFT. See ABBREVIATIONS, FIGURES.

ALIBI. An **alibi** is the proven fact of being elsewhere, not a false explanation.

ALTERNATE, as an adjective, means **every other**.

ALTERNATIVE: strictly, this is **one of two**, not one of three, four, five or more (which may be **options**).

AMEND is not quite the same as **emend**; though both result in an improvement, **emend** is used only of something written. **He amended his life by giving up gambling and drinking**, but **He emended his memo by correcting the spelling mistakes.**

AMERICANISMS. Use Americanisms discriminatingly. Many American words and expressions have passed into the language; others have vigour, particularly if used occasionally. Some are short and to the point. But many are unnecessarily long (so use **and** not **additionally, car** not **automobile, company** not **corporation, transport** not **transportation, district** not **neighbourhood, oblige** not **obligate, stocks** not **inventories** unless there is the risk of confusion with stocks and shares), the **army** not the **military**.

Grow a beard or a tomato but not a company. By all means **call for** a record profit if you wish to exhort the workers, but not if you merely predict one. Do not **post** it if it has been achieved. If it has not, look for someone new to **head** the company, not to **head it up**. Do not write **meet with** or **outside of**: **outside** America, you just **meet** people.

Try not to verb nouns or to adjective them. So do not **access** files, **haemorrhage** red ink (**haemorrhage** is a noun), let one event **impact** another, **author** books (still less **co-author** them), **critique** style sheets, **source** vegetables, **host** parties, **progress** reports, or **loan** money. **Gunned down** means **shot**.

Choose tenses according to British usage. In particular, do not fight shy of the perfect tense, especially where no date or time is given. Thus **Mr Bush has woken up to the danger** is preferable to **Mr Bush woke up to the danger**, unless you can add **last week** or **when he heard the explosion**.

Americans generally put the adverbs before the verb; the British put them after, as in normal speech. See also PART II.

AMID: use this instead of **amidst**.

AMONGST: prefer **among**.

AMPERSANDS. Ampersands should be used:

1. when they form part of the name of a company, like **AT&T**, **Pratt & Whitney**;
2. for such things as constituencies or other compound names where two names are linked to form one unit. **The rest of Brighouse & Spenborough joined with the Batley part of Batley & Morley to form Batley & Spen**. Or **The area thus became the Pakistani province of Kashmir and the Indian state of Jammu & Kashmir**;

3. in **R&D**, **M&A** and **S&L**.

AN should be used before a word beginning with a vowel sound (**an egg, an umbrella, an MP**) or an h if the h is silent. So **a hospital, a hotel**, but **an honorary degree, a European, a university, a U-turn.**

ANARCHY means the **complete absence of law** or government. It may be harmonious or chaotic.

ANIMALS, PLANTS, ETC. When it is necessary to use a Latin name, follow the standard practice. Thus for all creatures higher than viruses, write the binomial name in italics, giving an initial capital to the first word (the genus): ***Turdus turdus***, the song thrush; ***Metasequoia glyptostroboides***, the dawn redwood. Also ***Homo sapiens*** and cod uses such as ***Homo economicus***. On second mention, abbreviate the genus (***T. turdus***). In some species, like dinosaurs, the genus alone is used in lieu of a common name: ***Diplodocus***, ***Tyrannosaurus***. Also ***Drosophila***, a fruitfly favoured by geneticists. But ***Escherichia coli***, a bacterium also favoured by geneticists, is known universally as ***E. coli***, even on first mention.

ANTICIPATE does not mean **expect**. Jack and Jill expected to marry; if they anticipated marriage, only Jill might find herself expectant.

ANY ONE refers to a number; **anyone** to anybody.

ANY WAY refers to any manner; **anyway** means **nevertheless.**

APPEAL is intransitive nowadays (except in America), so **appeal against** decisions.

APPRAISE means **set a price on. Apprise** means **inform.**

AS OF (April 5th or April): prefer **on** (or **after**, or **since**) April 5th, **in** April.

AS TO: there is usually a more appropriate preposition.

AU. Astronomical unit. 1AU = distance from the sun to the earth.

AUTARCHY means **absolute sovereignty**; **autarky** means **self-sufficiency.**

B

BALE: in boats and in the hayfield, yes, otherwise **bail, bail out.**

BEG THE QUESTION means neither **invite** (or **raise**) **the question** nor **evade the answer.** To **beg the question** is to base a conclusion upon an assumption that is as much in need of proof as the conclusion itself. **All governments should promote free trade because otherwise protectionism will increase. This begs the question.**

BELLWETHER. This is the leading sheep of the flock, on whose neck a bell is hung. It has nothing to do with climate, prevailing winds or the like.

BIANNUAL can mean **twice a year** or **once every two years.** Avoid.

BIENNIAL also means **once in two years,** so is best avoided too.

BICENTENNIAL: prefer **bicentenary** (as a noun).

BILLION: a thousand million (abbreviated to **bn**). See also FIGURES.

BLACK. In the black means **in profit** in Britain, but **making losses** in some places. Always use **in profit.**

BOTH ... AND. A preposition placed after **both** should be repeated after **and.** Thus, **both to right and to left**; but **to both right and left** is all right.

Apply the same rule to **either ... or ... , neither ... nor ...** and **not only ... but (also) ...**

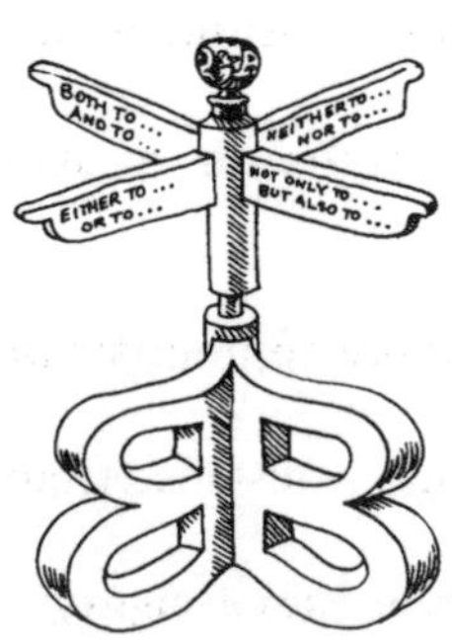

BROKERAGE is what a stockbroking firm does, not what it is.

C

Canute's exercise on the seashore aimed to persuade his courtiers of what he knew to be true but they doubted, that he was not omnipotent. Don't imply he was surprised to get his feet wet.

Capitals.

A balance has to be struck between so many capitals that the eyes dance and so few that the reader is diverted more by style than by substance. The general rule is to dignify with capital letters organisations and institutions, but not people. More exact rules are laid out below. Even these, however, leave some decisions to individual judgment. If in doubt use lower case unless it looks absurd. And remember that "a foolish consistency is the hobgoblin of little minds" (Ralph Waldo Emerson).

1. *People*

Use upper case for ranks and titles when written in conjunction with a name, but lower case when on their own. Thus, **President Bush**, but the **president**; **Vice-President Cheney**, but the **vice-president**; **Colonel Qaddafi** but the **colonel**; **Pope John Paul**, but the **pope**; **Queen Elizabeth**, but the **queen**.

Do not write **Prime Minister Blair** or **Defence Secretary Rumsfeld**; they are the **prime minister, Mr Blair**, and the **defence secretary, Mr Rumsfeld**. But you may write **Chancellor Schröder**.

All office holders when referred to merely by their office, not by their name, are lower case: the **chancellor of the exchequer**, the **foreign secretary**, the **prime minister**, the **speaker**, the **treasury secretary**, the **president of the United States**, the **chairman of British Coal**.

The only exceptions are: (a) a few titles that would look unduly peculiar without capitals, eg, **Black Rod**, **Master of the Rolls**, **Chancellor of the Duchy of Lancaster**, **Lord Privy Seal**, **Lord Chancellor**; (b) a few exalted people, such as the **Dalai Lama** and the **Aga Khan**. Also **God**. See also TITLES.

2. Organisations, ministries, departments, treaties, acts

These generally take upper case when their full name (or something pretty close to it, eg, **State Department**) is used. Thus, **European Commission**, **Forestry Commission**, **Arab League**, **Amnesty International**, the **Household Cavalry**, **Ministry of Agriculture**, **Department of Trade and Industry**, **Treasury**, **Metropolitan Police**, **High Court**, **Supreme Court**, **Court of Appeal**, **Senate**, **Central Committee**, **Politburo**, **Oxford University**, the **New York Stock Exchange** (but the **London stock exchange**, since that is only its informal name), the **Treaty of Rome**, the **Health and Safety at Work Act**, etc.

So, too, the **Crown**, the **House of Commons**, **House of Lords**, **House of Representatives**, **St Paul's Cathedral** (the **cathedral**), **World Bank** (the **Bank**), **Bank of England** (the **Bank**), **Department of State** (the **department**).

But organisations, committees, commissions, special groups, etc, that are either impermanent, ad hoc, local or relatively insignificant should be lower case. Thus: the **subcommittee on journalists' rights of the National Executive Committee of the Labour Party**, the **international economic subcommittee of the Senate Foreign Relations Committee**, the **Oxford University bowls club**, **Market Blandings rural district council**.

Use lower case for rough descriptions (the **Glass-Steagall act**, the **safety act**, the **American health department**, the **French parliament** as distinct from its **National Assembly**). If you are not sure whether the English translation of a foreign name is exact or not, assume it is rough and use lower case.

Parliament and **Congress** are upper case. But the **opposition** is lower case, even when used in the sense of **her majesty's loyal opposition**. The **government**, the **administration** and the **cabinet** are always lower case.

Exceptions

In finance and government there are some particular exceptions to the general rule of initial caps for full names, lower case for informal ones. Use caps for the **World Bank** and the **Fed** (after first spelling it out as the **Federal Reserve**), although these are shortened, informal names. The **Bank of England** and its foreign equivalents have initial capitals when named formally and separately, but collectively they are central banks in lower case (except those like Brazil's and Ireland's, which are actually named the **Central Bank**). **Special drawing rights** are lower case but abbreviated in small caps as **SDRs**, except when used with a figure as a currency (**SDR500m**). **Deutschmarks** will still probably be known just as **D-marks**, even when all references are historical. Treasury bonds issued by America's Treasury should be upper case; treasury bills (or bonds) of a general kind should be lower case. Avoid **T-bonds** and **t-bills.**

After first mention, the **House of Commons** (or **Lords**, or **Representatives**) becomes the **House**, the **World Bank** and **Bank of England** become the **Bank** and the **IMF** can become the **Fund.** Organisations with unusual names, such as the **African National Congress, Civic Forum** and the **European Union**, become the **Congress**, the **Forum** and the **Union**. But most other organisations, agencies, banks, commissions (including the **European Commission**), etc, take lower case when referred to incompletely on second and subsequent mentions.

3. *Political parties*

The full name of political parties is upper case, including the word party: **Republican Party, Labour Party, Peasants' Party, Conservative Party.** Note that usually only people are **Democrats, Christian Democrats, Liberal Democrats** or **Social Democrats**; their parties, policies, committees, etc, are **Democratic, Christian Democratic, Liberal Democratic** or **Social Democratic** (although a committee may be **Democrat-controlled**). An exception is Britain's **Liberal Democrat Party**.

When referring to a specific party, write **Labour**, the **Republican nominee**, a prominent **Liberal**, etc, but use lower case in looser references to **liberals, conservatism, communists**, etc. **Tories**, however, are upper case, as are true **Communists.** And **the left** and **the right** are lower case.

4. *Labels formed from proper names*

A political, economic or religious label formed from a proper name should have a capital. Thus **Gaullism, Paisleyite, Leninist, Napoleonic, Luddite, Marxist, Hobbesian, Christian, Buddhism, Hindu, Islamic, Maronite, Finlandisation, Thatcherism.**

5. *Places*

Use initial capitals for definite geographical places, regions, areas, countries and buildings (**The Hague, Transylvania, Germany**, the

Foreign Office), and for vague but recognised political or geographical areas: the **Middle East**, **North** and **South Atlantic**, **East Asia** (which is to be preferred to the **Far East**), the **West** (as in the decline of the **West**), the **Gulf**, **South-East Asia**, the **Midlands**, **Central America**, the **West Country**, the **Highlands** (of Scotland).

Compass points
Use lower case for **east**, **west**, **north**, **south** except when part of a name (**North Korea**, **South Africa**, **West End**, **Central**, **South** and **South-east Asia**) or when part of a thinking group: the **South** (in the United States), the **North-South divide**. But use lower case if you are, say, comparing regions of the United States, some of which are merely geographical areas: **House prices in the north-east and the south are rising faster than those in the mid-west and the south-west.**

Use **West Germany (Berlin)** and **East Germany (Berlin)** only in historical references. They are now **western Germany (western Berlin)** and **eastern Germany (eastern Berlin).**

Lower case
The **third world** (an unsatisfactory term now that the communist second world has disappeared) is lower case.

Use lower case for province, river, state, city when not strictly part of the name: the **Limpopo river**, **Washington state**, **New York state**, **Cabanas province**. But the **River Thames**, **Mississippi River**, and **Guatemala City**, **Ho Chi Minh City**, **Kuwait City**, **Mexico City**, **New York City**, **Panama City** and **Quebec City**, even though **City** is not part of their proper names, as it is in **Dodge City**, **Kansas City**, **Oklahoma City**, **Quexon City**, **Salt Lake City**).

If in doubt, use lower case (**the sunbelt**).

6. Avoiding confusion
Use capitals to avoid confusion, especially with no (and therefore yes). **In Bergen no votes predominated** suggests a stalemate, whereas **In Bergen No votes predominated** suggests a triumph of noes over yeses. In most contexts, though, yes and no should be lower case: "The answer is no."

7. Euro-terms
Usual rules apply for the full, proper names and their informal use.
European Commission, the **commission**
European Parliament, the **parliament**
Treaty of Rome, the **Rome treaty**
Treaty on European Union, the **Maastricht treaty**

The **European Union** becomes the **Union** after first mention.

An IGC is an **inter-governmental conference**, the CAP is the **common agricultural policy** and EMU is **economic and monetary union**. When making **Euro-** or **euro-words**, introduce a hyphen, except for **Europhile, Europhobe** and **Eurosceptic** (and their **euro-equivalents**). Prefer **euro zone** or **euro area** to **euro-land.** See also CURRENCIES.

8. e-expressions

The **internet**, the **net**; **world wide web**, the **web, website**. See also E-EXPRESSIONS, page 27.

9. *Historical periods* (upper case)

Black Death
Cultural Revolution
the Depression
Middle Ages
New Deal
Renaissance
Restoration
Year of the Dog

10. *Trade names* (upper case)

Hoover, Teflon, Valium, Walkman.

11. *Miscellaneous* (upper case)

the Bar
Catholics
Coloureds (in South Africa)
Christmas, Labour, May and New Year's Day, Christmas Eve, New Year's Eve
Cup Final
Davis Cup
Hispanics
House of Laity
Koran
Kyoto protocol
Koran
Latinos
Mafia (the genuine article)
Protestants
the Queen's speech
Russify
Semitic (-ism), anti-Semitism
Social Security (American usage)
the Speaker
Stealth fighter, bomber, missile
Teamster
Test match
Utopia (-n)
Utopia (-n)

12. *Miscellaneous* (lower case)

19th amendment (but Article 19)
aborigines
anglicised
blacks
civil servant, service
cold war
common market
constitution
cruise missile
draconian
first, second world war (and names of most wars, but not Gulf war)

francophone
french windows
general synod
industrial revolution
mafia (any old group of criminals)
mid-west
new year
philistine
platonic
the press
quixotic
realpolitik
state-of-the-union message
titanic
tsar
white paper
wild west
young turk

CARTEL. A cartel is a group that restricts supply in order to drive up prices. Do not use it to describe any old syndicate or association of producers – especially of drugs.

CASE. "There is perhaps no single word so freely resorted to as a trouble-saver," says Gowers, "and consequently responsible for so much flabby writing." Often you can do without it. **There are many cases of it being unnecessary** is better as **It is often unnecessary. If it is the case that** simply means **If. It is not the case** means **It is not so.**

CASSANDRA'S predictions were correct but not believed.

CATALYST. This is something that speeds up a chemical reaction while itself remaining unchanged. Do not confuse it with one of the agents.

CENSOR. The critics may **censure** a bad play, but oppose any attempt to **censor** it, that is **suppress all or part** of it.

CENTRED on, not **around** or **in.**

CHARGE. If you **charge** intransitively, do so as a bull, cavalry officer or some such, not as an **accuser**. So avoid **The standard of writing was abysmal, he charged.**

CIRCUMSTANCES stand **around** a thing, so it is **in**, not **under**, them.

COLLAPSE is not a transitive verb. You may collapse, but you may not collapse something.

COLLECTIVE NOUNS. There is no firm rule about the number of a verb governed by a singular collective noun. It is best to go by the sense. This applies whether the collective noun stands for a single entity: **The council was elected in March, The me generation has run its course, The staff is loyal**; or for its constituents: **The council are at**

sixes and sevens over taxes, The preceding generation are all dead, The staff are at each other's throats.

A rule for **number: The number is ... , A number are ...**

A pair and **a couple** are both plural.

Majority: when it is used in an abstract sense, it takes the singular; when it is used to denote the elements making up the majority, it should be plural. **A two-thirds majority is needed to amend the constitution** but **A majority of the Senate were opposed.**

A **government**, a **party**, a **company** (whether Tesco or Marks and Spencer) and a **partnership** (Skidmore, Owings & Merrill) are all **it**, and take a singular verb. Brokers are singular: **Legg Mason Wood Walk is preparing a statement.** Avoid usages such as **bankers Chase Manhattan** or **accountants Ernst & Young**. And remember that **Barclays** is a **British bank**, not **the British bank**, just as **Ford** is **a car company**, not **the car company**. And **Luciano Pavarotti** is **an opera singer**, not **the opera singer**.

A **country** is **it**, and takes a singular verb, even if its name looks plural. Thus **The Philippines has a congressional system, as does the United States; the Netherlands does not.** The **United Nations** is singular.

Acoustics, ballistics, classics, dynamics, economics, ethics, kinetics, mathematics, mechanics, physics, politics and **statics** are singular when being used generally, without the definite article. Thus **Economics is the dismal science, Politics is the art of the possible** (Bismarck).

But such **-ics** words are plural when preceded by **the**, or **the** plus an adjective, or with a possessive. **The politics of Afghanistan have a logic all their own, The dynamics of the dynasty were dynamite, The economics of publishing are uncertain. Antics, atmospherics, basics, graphics, heroics, histrionics, hysterics, tactics** and **statistics** are all plural. **Specifics** are discouraged (try **details**).

Some nouns ending in **s** are always treated as singular; they include **news** and games such as **darts, bowls, fives** and **billiards.**

Terms that take the name of a town, country or university are plural, even when they work singularly: **England were bowled out for 56.**

Prefer the singular when dealing with **chemical** (not **chemicals**) companies, **drug** (not **drugs**) traffickers, **pension** (not **pensions**) **systems** and so on. But **arms-trader** and **sales force.**

Law and order defies the rules of grammar and is singular.

Come up with: try **suggest, originate** or **produce.**

Commit. Do not **commit to**, but by all means **commit yourself to** something.

COMPANIES.
Call companies by the names they call themselves.

Accenture
Airbus
Allied Domecq
American Telephone and Telegraph (AT&T)
Anglo American
AOL Time Warner
AstraZeneca
BAE Systems
Bank of Tokyo-Mitsubishi
Bank One
British American Tobacco
Benetton
Bertelsmann
Bloomingdale's
BNP Paribas
Boots (the chemist)
Bouygues
BSkyB
Cadbury Schweppes
Coca-Cola
Conoco
Credit Suisse
Cummins
DaimlerChrysler
Diageo
Dresdner Kleinwort Wasserstein (DKW)
DuPont
Eastman Kodak
Ericsson
Ernst & Young
Exxon Mobil
Fannie Mae
GlaxoSmithKline
Goldman Sachs
Harrods
Hewlett-Packard
Kmart
Kohlberg Kravis Roberts
Levi Strauss
Lloyd's (insurance market)
Lloyds TSB (the bank)
Lord & Taylor
McDonald's
Marks & Spencer
Merck
Merrell
Merrill Lynch
Messerschmitt-Bölkow-Blohm (MBB)
Moët & Chandon
Moody's
J.P. Morgan Chase
Nippon Telegraph and Telephone (NTT)
Novell
NTT DoCoMo
People's Bank (South African bank)
Pfizer
Philips
Pillsbury
PolyGram
Pratt & Whitney
PricewaterhouseCoopers
Procter & Gamble
Reuters (adjective Reuter)
Rolls-Royce
Saks Fifth Avenue
Sears, Roebuck
Standard & Poor's
ThyssenKrupp
Toys "R" Us
Unisys
Unix
Vodafone Group
Wal-Mart
Weyerhaeuser
Yahoo!

COMPARE. A is compared **with** B when you draw attention to the difference. A is compared **to** B when you want to stress their similarity ("Shall I compare thee to a summer's day?").

COMPLAISANT people aim to please others; if they are **complacent**, they are pleased with themselves.

COMPOUND does not mean **make worse**. It may mean **combine** or, intransitively, **agree** or **come to terms**. To **compound a felony** means to **agree for a consideration not to prosecute**.

COMPRISE means **is composed of**. **The Democratic coalition comprises women, workers, blacks and Jews. Women make up** (not comprise) **three-fifths of the Democratic coalition** or, **Three-fifths of the Democratic coalition is composed of women.**

CONTINUOUS describes something uninterrupted; **continual** admits of a break. If your neighbours play loud music every night, it is a **continual nuisance**; it is not a **continuous nuisance** unless the music is never turned off.

CONVINCE. Don't **convince** people to do something. In that context the word you want is **persuade**. **The prime minister was persuaded to call a June election; he was convinced of the wisdom of doing so only after he had won.**

COUNTRIES AND THEIR INHABITANTS. In most contexts favour simplicity over precision and use **Britain** rather than **Great Britain** or the **United Kingdom**, and **America** rather than the **United States of America**. ("In all pointed sentences some degree of accuracy must be sacrificed to conciseness." Dr Johnson.) See also page 27 and pages 152ff.

Sometimes, however, it may be important to be precise. Remember therefore that **Great Britain** consists of **England**, **Scotland** and **Wales**, which together with **Northern Ireland** (which we generally call **Ulster**, though Ulster strictly includes three counties in the republic of Ireland) make up the **United Kingdom (UK)**.

Ireland is simply **Ireland**. Although it is a republic, it is not the Republic of Ireland. Neither is it, in English, Eire.

Holland, though a nice, short, familiar name, is strictly only two of the 12 provinces that make up **the Netherlands**, and the **Dutch** are increasingly indignant about misuse of the shorter name. So use **the Netherlands**.

The primary definition of **Scandinavia** is Norway and Sweden, but it is often used to include Denmark, Iceland, Norway and Sweden, which, with Finland, make up the **Nordic countries.**

Where countries have made it clear that they wish to be called by a new (or an old) name, respect their requests. Thus **Côte d'Ivoire, Myanmar, Burkina Faso, Congo** (there are two), **Sri Lanka, Thailand, Zimbabwe.** See also PLACES, pages 52–54.

The former **Soviet Union** used often to be called **Russia**, particularly in foreign-policy contexts. But Russia today is the largest and most important of the countries that make up the COMMONWEALTH OF INDEPENDENT STATES, which has 12 members, including Belarus (not Belorussia), Kazakhstan, Kirgizstan (not Kirgizia or Kyrgyzstan), Moldova (not Moldavia), Tajikistan, Turkmenistan (not Turkmenia) and Uzbekistan (see pages 144, 154).

Remember, too, that although it is usually all right to talk about the inhabitants of the United States as **Americans**, the term also applies to everyone from Canada to Cape Horn. It may sometimes be necessary to write **United States citizens.** Do not use **US**, except where it is part of a company's name, or with currencies. In all cases it is best to refer to the specific nationality: thus **Canadians** rather than **North Americans.** (See also EUROPEAN UNION, page 27.)

CREDIBLE means to **be believable; credulous** means **too ready to believe. Her explanation for missing the meeting was credible. His explanation that he found the money at the end of the rainbow convinced only the credulous.**

CRESCENDO. This is not an acme, apogee, summit or zenith but a **passage of increasing loudness.** You cannot therefore **build to a crescendo.**

CRISIS. This is a decisive event or turning-point. Many of the economic and political troubles wrongly described as **crises** are really **persistent difficulties, sagas** or **affairs.**

CRITIQUE is a noun. If you want a verb, try **criticise.**

CURRENCIES. Use $ as the standard currency and in general convert currencies to $ on first mention. See also CURRENCIES; FIGURES; MEASUREMENTS; and MEASURES.

Britain

1p, 2p, 3p, to **99p** (*not* £0.99)
£6 (*not* £6.00)
£5,000–6000 (*not* £5,000–£6,000)
£5m–6m (*not* £5m–£6m)
£5 billion–6 billion (*not* £5–6 billion)

America
$ will do generally. Spell out **cents.**

Other dollars include **A$** (Australian dollars), **C$** (Canadian dollars), **HK$** (Hong Kong dollars), **M$** (Malaysian dollars), **NT$** (New Taiwan dollars), **NZ$** (New Zealand dollars) and **S$** (Singapore dollars).

Sums in certain currencies are written in full, with the number first: **100m ecus,** 100**m kwacha, 100m liras** (Turkish), **100m naira, 100m rand** (not rands), **100m rupees** and **100m renminbi.** With other currencies, such as **SDR, DKr** (Danish krone, kroner), **Y** (yen) and **€** (euro), write the abbreviation followed by the figure: **SDR1m, DKr1,000, Y1,000, €2,000.** Currencies such as **DM, FFr** and **BFr** will soon crop up only in historical references.

To avoid confusion the Brazilian ***real*** (plural ***reais***) is set in italics.

For a full list of currencies and currency symbols, see pages 113–117.

Current and **contemporary** mean **at that time,** not necessarily **at this time.** So a series of **current prices** from 1960 to 1970 will not be in **today's prices,** just as **contemporary art** in 1800 was not **modern art. Contemporary history** is a contradiction in terms.

D

DATA are plural.

DATES. Month, day, year, in that order, with no commas:

July 5th	**July 2003**
Monday July 5th	**1990s, 2000s**
July 5th 2003	**July 27th–August 3rd 2003**
July 5th–12th 2003	**1998–99, 2000–01**

Write
11th century, 21st century, but **first to tenth centuries**
21st-century ideas
a man in his 20s, and **20th anniversary**
a 29-year-old, a 29-year-old man
in 100 years' time

Do not write **on June 10th–14th**. Prefer **between June 10th and 14th.** If, say, ministers are going to meet over two days, write **December 14th and 15th**, not **December 14th–15th.**

In general give dates; **last week** or **last month** can cause confusion.

See also FIGURES and HYPHENS.

DECIMATE means to destroy a proportion (originally a tenth) of a group of people or things, not to destroy them all or nearly all.

DEFINITIVE means authoritative, final, decisive; **definite** means precise, distinct.

DELIVER is transitive. So if someone is to **deliver**, he must deliver **letters, babies** or **the goods** – whether **groceries** or **what he promised.**

DEMOGRAPHICS. No, the word is **demography**.

DEPRECATE means to **express disapproval of; depreciate** means to **belittle** or **reduce the value of. They deprecated his violent language but did not wish to depreciate the importance of his message.**

DIFFERENT from, not **to** or **than.**

DILEMMA. This is not any old awkwardness, it is one with horns, being, properly, a form of argument (the horned syllogism) in which you find yourself committed to accept one of two propositions, each of which contradicts your original contention. So a dilemma offers the choice between alternatives, each with equally nasty consequences.

Discreet means **circumspect** or **prudent; discrete** means **separate** or **distinct**. Remember that **"Questions are never indiscreet. Answers sometimes are."** (Oscar Wilde)

Disinterested means **impartial; uninterested** means **bored. ("Disinterested curiosity is the lifeblood of civilisation."** G.M. Trevelyan.)

Distinctive means **characteristic, serving to identify; distinct** means **definite, distinguishable, separate. Entering his room, she noticed that, as well as the distinctive smell of the cigars he always smoked, there was a faint but distinct odour of rotting fish.**

Due to has three meanings:

1. caused by, as in **The cancellation, due to rain, of ...** In this sense, it must follow a noun, so do not write **The match was cancelled due to rain**. If you mean **because of** and for some reason are reluctant to say it, you probably want **owing to. It was cancelled owing to rain** is all right.
2. owed to, as in **A month's salary is due to Smith.**
3. arranged or timed to, as in **The meeting is due to end at 3.30.**

E

E-. The prefix **e-** stands for electronic, and is combined with many expressions. See E-EXPRESSIONS, CAPITALS.

-EABLE. See -ABLE.

EARNINGS. Do not write **earnings** when you mean **profits** (say if they are operating, gross, pre-tax or net).

-EE: employees, evacuees, detainees, referees, refugees but, please, no **attendees** (those attending), **draftees** (conscripts), **escapees** (escapers), **retirees** (the retired), or **standees.** A **divorcee** may be male or female.

E-EXPRESSIONS. The "e-" is lower case and hyphenated: **e-business, e-commerce, e-mail.** Computer technology terms are also lower case: **dotcom, online, laptop, the net** (and **internet**), the **web, website** and **world wide web.**

Cyber-terms are also lower case: **cyber-attack, cyber-soccer, cybernetics, cyberspace, cyberwars.**

CD-ROM is in small capitals.

EFFECT, the verb, means to **accomplish,** so **The novel effected a change in his attitude.** See also AFFECT.

EFFECTIVELY means **with effect**; if you mean **in effect**, say it. **The matter was effectively dealt with on Friday** means it was **done well** on Friday. **The matter was, in effect, dealt with on Friday** means that it was **more or less attended to** on Friday. **Effectively leaderless** would do as a description of the demonstrators in East Germany in 1989 but not those in Tiananmen Square. The devaluation of the Slovak currency in 1993, described by some as an **effective** 8%, turned out to be a rather ineffective 8%.

EITHER ... OR. See NONE.

ELECTIONS are not always plural. **The opposition demanded an election** is often preferable to **The opposition demanded fresh elections.**

ENORMITY means a **crime, sin** or **monstrous wickedness.** It does not mean immensity.

ENVIRONMENT. Often unavoidable, but not a pretty word. Avoid the **business environment**, the **school environment** and the **work environment**. Try to rephrase the sentence: **business conditions, at school, at work. Surroundings** is often better.

EPICENTRE means that point on the earth's surface above the centre of an earthquake. To say that **Mr Jones was at the epicentre of the dispute** suggests that the argument took place underground.

ETHNIC GROUPS. Avoid giving offence. This should be your first concern. But also avoid mealy-mouthed euphemisms and terms that have not generally caught on despite promotion by pressure-groups. If American blacks do not wish to be called **black**, as some years ago it became plain that they no longer wished to be called **coloured**, call them **African-American** (or whatever is correct). Till then they are called **blacks.**

When writing about Spanish-speaking people in the United States, use **Latino** or **Hispanic** as a general term, but try to be specific (eg, **Mexican-American**).

Africans may be black or white. If you mean blacks, write **blacks.** In South Africa people of mixed race are **Coloureds.**

The inhabitants of **Azerbaijan** are **Azerbaijanis**, some of whom, but not all, are **Azeris**. Those **Azeris** who live in other places, such as Iran, are not **Azerbaijanis**. Similarly, many **Croats** are not **Croatian**, and many **Serbs** not **Serbian.**

Anglo-Saxon is not a synonym for English-speaking.

The language spoken in Iran and Tajikistan is **Persian**, not **Farsi. Flemings** speak **Dutch.**

See also STATES, pages 152ff.

EUROPEAN UNION. Can be abbreviated to EU or the **Union** after first mention. **Europe** and **Europeans** may be used as shorthand for citizens of the countries of the EU, but be careful for there are plenty of other Europeans too. See also COUNTRIES AND THEIR INHABITANTS, pages 21–22.

EURO-TERMS. See page 16.

EVERY ONE refers to a number; **everyone** means **everybody.**

EX. Be careful: **a Liberal ex-member** has lost his seat; **an ex-Liberal member** has lost his party.

EXCEPTIONABLE means **can be taken exception to; exceptional** means

unusual, out of the ordinary. To claim that there has been no musical genius since Beethoven is an exceptionable remark, as there have been many other exceptional composers.

EXECUTE means put to death by law. Do not use it as a synonym for **murder. An extra-judicial execution** is a contradiction in terms.

F

FACT. The fact that can usually be boiled down to **that.**

FALSE POSSESSIVE. Try to avoid usages such as **London's Heathrow Airport.**

FEWER (not **less**) **than seven speeches, fewer than seven samurai.** Use **fewer**, not **less**, with numbers of individual items or people. **Less than £200, less than 700 tonnes of oil, less than a third**, because these are measured quantities or proportions, not individual items.

FIEF, not **fiefdom.**

FIGURES. Never start a sentence with a figure; write the number in words instead.

Use figures for numerals from 11 upwards, and for all numerals that include a decimal point or a fraction (eg, **4.25, 4¼**). Use words for simple numerals from one to ten, except: in references to pages; in percentages (eg, **4%**); and in sets of numerals some of which are higher than ten, eg, **Deaths from this cause in the past three years were 14, 9 and 6.** It is occasionally permissible to use words rather than numbers when referring to a rough or rhetorical figure (such as **a thousand curses**).

Use **m** for **million.** But spell out **billion,** except in charts, where **bn** is permissible. Thus: **8m, £8m, 8 billion, DKr8 billion.**

A **billion** is a thousand million, a **trillion** a thousand billion (or a million million, abbreviated as **trn**), a **quadrillion** a thousand trillion. See also METRIC SYSTEM PREFIXES, page 134.

Use **5,000–6,000** and **5–6%; 5m–6m** (not **5–6m**), **$5m–6m;** and **5 billion–6 billion** or **5bn–6bn.** But **sales rose from 5m to 6m** (not **5m–6m**); **estimates ranged between 5m and 6m** (not **5m–6m**).

Where **to** is being used as part of a ratio, it is usually best to spell it out. Thus **They decided, by nine votes to two, to put the matter to the general assembly which voted, 27 to 19, to insist that the ratio of vodka to tomato juice in a bloody mary should be at least one to three, though the odds of this being so in most bars were put at no better than 11 to 4.** Where a ratio is being used adjectivally, figures and hyphens may be used, but only if one of the figures is greater than ten: thus, a **50-20 vote.** Otherwise, spell out the figures and use **to: a two-to-one vote.**

Do not use a hyphen or dash in place of **to** except with figures: **He**

received a sentence of 15–20 years in jail but **He promised to have escaped within three to four weeks' time.**

Avoid **from 1996–99** (say **in 1996–99** or **from 1996 to 1999**) and **between 1996–99** (say **in 1996–99** or **from 1996 to 1999**).

Avoid Latin with figures. Use **a person** or **per person, a year** or **per year**, not **per caput, per capita** or **per annum.**

See also HYPHENS; MEASUREMENTS; MEASURES.

Percentages

Use the sign **%** instead of **per cent.** But write **percentage**, not **%age** (though in most contexts **proportion** or **share** is preferable). See also PER CENT.

Fractions

Fractions should be hyphenated (**two-thirds, five-eighths**, etc) and, unless they are attached to whole numbers (**8½, 29⅝**), spelled out in words, even when the figures are higher than ten: **He gave one-tenth of his salary to the church, one-twentieth to his mistress and one-thirtieth to his wife**, although in non-numerical contexts it may be permissible to write, for example, **a tenth of his income.** See also FRACTIONS, page 121.

Do not compare a fraction with a decimal (so avoid **The rate fell from 3½% to 3.1%**).

You should use fractions for rough figures (**Kenya's population is growing at 3½% a year, A hectare is 2½ acres**) and decimals for more exact ones: **The retail price index is rising at an annual rate of 10.6%.** Treat all numbers with respect. Beware of phoney over-precision like more than one decimal place. Favour rounding off.

Aircraft

The style for aircraft types can be confusing. Some have hyphens in obvious places (eg, **DC-10, F-22, B-2 bombers**), some in unusual places (**MiG-31M, MiG-29SMT**) and some none at all (**Airbus A340, BAe, RJ70**). For Boeing, write Boeing 747, etc. Other aircraft have both name and number (**Lockheed P-3 Orion**). When in doubt, use Jane's "All The World's Aircraft". Its index includes makers' correct names. See also HYPHENS.

Calibres

The style for calibres is **50mm** or **105mm** with no hyphen; but **5.5-inch** and **25-pounder.**

FINALLY. Do not use **finally** when, at the end of a series, you mean

lastly or, in other contexts, when you mean **at last. Richard Burton finally marries Liz Taylor** would have been all right second time round but not first.

FLAUNT means **display; flout** means **disdain.** If you **flout** this distinction you will **flaunt** your ignorance.

FOCUS. All the world's a stage, not a lens.

FOREIGN WORDS AND PHRASES. Try not to use foreign words and phrases unless there is no English alternative, which is unusual (so **a year** or **per year**, not **per annum; a person** or **per person** not **per capita; beyond one's authority** not **ultra vires;** etc). See also ITALICS and LATIN.

FOR EVER: for all time; **forever** means **unceasingly**.

FORGO means **do without;** it forgoes the **e. Forego** means **go before. A foregone conclusion** is one that is predetermined; **a forgone conclusion** is non-existent.

FORMER: avoid wherever possible use of **the former** and **the latter**. It usually causes confusion. (See also EX.)

FORTUITOUS means **accidental**, not **fortunate** or **well-timed.**

FRACTIONS. See pages 30, 121.

FRACTIOUS means **peevish** or **unruly; factious** means **divisive** or produced by **faction. English soccer fans have a reputation for being both fractious and factious.**

FRANKENSTEIN was not a monster, but his creator.

FREE is an adjective or an adverb, so you cannot have or do anything **for free.** Either you have it **free** or you have it **for nothing.**

FUND is a technical term, meaning to **convert floating debt into more or less permanent debt at fixed interest.** Do not use it if you mean to **finance** or to **pay for.**

G

Garner means **store**, not **gather**.

Gender is a word to be applied to grammar, not people. If someone is female, that is her **sex** not her **gender**.

Generation: take care. You can be a second-generation Frenchman, but if you are a second-generation immigrant that means you have left the country your parents came to.

Genitive. Take care with the genitive. It is fine to say **a friend of John's**, just as you would say **a friend of mine**, so you can also say **a friend of John's and Jane's.** But it is also fine to say **a friend of John**, or **a friend of John and Jane.** What you must not say is **John and Jane's friend.** If you wish to use that construction, you must say **John's and Jane's friend**, which is cumbersome.

Gentlemen's agreement, not **gentleman's.**

Gerund. Respect the gerund. Gerunds look like participles – **running, jumping, standing** – but are more noun-like, and should never therefore be preceded by a personal pronoun. So the following are wrong: **I was awoken by him snoring. Please forgive me coming late.** Those sentences should have ended: **his snoring, my coming late.** In other words, use the possessive adjective rather than the personal pronoun.

Get: an adaptable verb, but it has its limits. A man does not **get** sacked or promoted, he **is** sacked or promoted.

Gourmet means **epicure; gourmand** means **greedy-guts.**

H

Halve is a transitive verb, so deficits can double but not **halve.** They must **be halved** or **fall by half.**

Hanging clauses. If you begin a sentence with an adjectival or adverbial phrase, make sure that it qualifies the subject of the sentence. Thus, avoid: **After a fortnight's absence, your house plants will have shrivelled up.** See also pages 2–3 on sloppy sentences.

Haver means to **talk nonsense**, not **dither** or **waver.**

Healthy. If you think something is **desirable** or **good**, say so. Do not call it **healthy.**

Hoards are secreted treasures, not multitudes on the move (**hordes**).

Hobson's choice is not **the lesser of two evils**, it is **no choice at all.**

Homogeneous means **of the same kind or nature. Homogenous** means **similar because of common descent.**

Homophobe means someone who dislikes HOMOSEXUALS.

Homosexual. Since this word comes from the Greek word *homos* (same), not the Latin word *homo* (man), it applies as much to women as to men. It is therefore as daft to write **homosexuals and lesbians** as to write **people and women.**

Hopefully. By all means begin an article hopefully, but never write: **Hopefully, it will be finished by Wednesday.** Try: **with luck, if all goes well, it is hoped that ...**

Hyphens. Use hyphens as follows.

1. ***Fractions***
Whether nouns or adjectives: **two-thirds, four-fifths, one-sixth**, etc. See also FRACTIONS, pages 30, 121.

2. ***Prefixes***
Most words that begin with prefixes like **anti, non** and **neo: anti-aircraft, anti-fascist, anti-submarine** (but **antibiotic, anticli-**

max, antidote, antiseptic, antitrust); non-combatant, non-existent, non-payment, non-violent (but **nonaligned, nonconformist, nonplussed, nonstop); neo-conservative, neo-liberal** (but **neoclassicism, neolithic, neologism).**

Hyphens are not necessary with the prefixes **over, under** and **sub.**

Some words that become unmanageable with an added prefix need hyphenating: **under-secretary** and **inter-governmental.**

Antidisestablishmentarianism would, however, lose its point it if were hyphenated.

A sum followed by the word **worth** also needs a hyphen: thus, **$25m-worth of goods.**

3. *Euro-terms*

Words that begin with **Euro** or **euro** should be hyphenated, except **Europhile, Europhobe** and **Eurosceptic**; euro zone, euro area. See also CAPITALS.

4. *Some titles*

vice-president	**lieutenant-colonel**	*but*
director-general	**major-general**	**deputy director**
under-secretary	**field-marshal**	**deputy secretary**
secretary-general		**district attorney**
attorney-general		**general secretary**

5. *To avoid ambiguities*

a little-used car **a little used-car**
cross-complaint **cross complaint**
high-school girl **high schoolgirl**
fine-tooth comb (most people do not comb their teeth)
third-world war **third world war**

6. *Adjectives formed from two or more words*

right-wing groups (but **the right wing** of the party)
balance-of-payments difficulties
private-sector wages
public-sector borrowing requirement
a 70-year-old judge
state-of-the-union message
value-added tax (VAT)

7. *Adverbs*

These do not need to be linked to participles or adjectives by hyphens in simple constructions: **The regiment was ill equipped** for its task; The principle is well established; Though expensively educated, the journalist knew no grammar.** But if the adverb is one of two words together being used adjectivally, a hyphen may be needed: **The ill-equipped regiment was soon repulsed; All well-established principles should be periodically challenged.** The hyphen is especially likely to be needed if the adverb is short and common, such as **ill**, **little**, **much** and **well.** Less-common adverbs, including all those that end -ly, are less likely to need hyphens: **Never employ an expensively educated journalist.** See ADVERBS.

8. Separating identical letters

Book-keeping (but **bookseller**), **coat-tails**, **co-operate**, **unco-operative**, **miss-spell**, **pre-eminent**, **pre-empt** (but **predate**, **precondition**), **re-emerge**, **re-entry** (but **rearm**, **rearrange**, **reborn**, **repurchase**), **trans-ship.**

Exceptions include **override**, **overrule**, **underrate**, **withhold.** See PREFIXES, pages 34–35.

9. Nouns formed from prepositional verbs

Bail-out, **build-up**, **buy-out**, **call-up**, **get-together**, **lay-off**, **pay-off**, **pull-out**, **round-up**, **set-up**, **shake-out**, **shake-up**, **stand-off**, **start-up**, etc. But **fallout**, **handout**, **payout**, **shutdown**, **turnout.**

10. The quarters of the compass

North-east(ern), **south-east(ern)**, **south-west(ern)**, **north-west(ern)**, **the mid-west(ern).**

11. Makers and other words ending -er: general rule

If the prefix is of one or two syllables, attach it without a hyphen to form a single word, but if the prefix is of three or more syllables, introduce a hyphen. So **carmaker**, **troublemaker** but **candlestick-maker. Policymaker** (one word) is an exception.

With other words ending **-er** that are similar to **maker** (**builder**, **dealer**, **driver**, **grower**, **owner**, **player**, **runner**, **seeker**, **trafficker**, **worker**, etc) the general rule should be to insert a hyphen. But some prefixes, especially those of one syllable, can be used to form single words (**coalminer**, **foxhunter**, **shipbroker**) and some combinations will be better left as two words (**insurance broker**, **tuba player**, **crossword compiler**).

12. *One word* (see also PREFIXES, pages 34–35)

airfield
bedfellow
bestselling
bilingual
blackboard
blueprint
businessman
bypass
ceasefire
coastguard
comeback
commonsense (adj)
cyberspace
figleaf
foothold
forever (adverb)
goodwill
halfhearted
handpicked
hardline
headache
hijack
hobnob
kowtow
lacklustre
landmine
laptop
loophole
lopsided
lukewarm
machinegun
multilingual
nationwide
nevertheless
nonetheless
offline
offshore
oilfield
online
onshore
peacetime
petrochemical
placename
proofread
rainforest
ringtone
roadblock
rustbelt
seabed
semiconductor
shortlist
shutdown
soyabean
spillover
statewide
stockmarket
strongman
sunbelt
takeover
threshold
timetable
transatlantic
transpacific
turnout
videocassette
videodisc
wartime
website
workforce
worldwide
worthwhile

13. *Two words*

ad hoc
air base
air force
any more
arm's length
ballot box
birth rate
cash flow
child care
chip maker
common sense (noun)
errand boy
for ever (after a verb)
girl friend
health care (noun)
Land Rover
microchip maker
no one
on to
sales force
some day
under way
vice versa

14. *Two words hyphenated*

agri-business
aid-worker
aircraft-carrier
asylum-seekers
catch-phrase
death-squads
drawing-board
end-game
end-year
faint-hearted
front-line
front-runner
hand-held
health-care (adj)
heir-apparent

hot-head
ice-cream
infra-red
interest-group
inter-governmental
joint-venture (adj)
kerb-crawler
know-how
like-minded
light-year
long-standing
machine-tool
mid-week, mid-August, etc
nation-building
nation-state
news-stand
post-war, pre-war
pressure-group
pull-out (noun)
question-mark
rain-check
re-create (create again)
re-present (present again)
re-sort (sort again)
starting-point
sticking-point
stumbling-block
talking-shop
task-force
tear-gas
think-tank
time-bomb
turning-point
vote-winner
working-party

15. *Three words*
ad hoc agreement, meeting, etc
armoured personnel carrier
capital gains tax
chiefs of staff
half a dozen
in as much
in so far
multiple rocket launcher
nuclear power station
nuclear aircraft carrier
third world war

16. *Three words hyphenated*
brother-in-law
chock-a-block
commander-in-chief
no-man's-land
prisoners-of-war
second-in-command

17. *Date ranges*
Avoid **from 1996–99** (say **in 1996–99** or **from 1996 to 1999**) and **between 1996–99** (say in **1996–99** or **from 1996 to 1999**). Some people use dashes, not hyphens, with dates. A hyphen (or dash) should not be used instead of **to** except with figures. See also DATES, FIGURES.

18. *Stringing together*
Do not overdo the literary device of hyphenating words not usually linked, **the stringing-together-of-lots-and-lots-of-words-and-ideas tendency**.

19. *Hybrid ethnics*
Greek-Cypriot, **Irish-American**, etc, whether noun or adjective.

HYPOTHERMIA is what kills old folk in winter. If you say it is **hyperthermia**, that means they have been carried off by heat stroke.

I

-IBLE. See -ABLE.

ILK means **same**, so **of that ilk** means **of the place of the same name as the family**, not **of that kind.** Best avoided.

IMMOLATE means to **sacrifice**, not to **burn.**

IMPORTANT. If something is important, say why and to whom; and use sparingly.

INCHOATE means **not fully developed** or **at an early stage**, and not **incoherent** or **chaotic**.

INFER. By including this word, we **imply** that it is sometimes misused. When reading this entry, you **infer** that the two highlighted words have different meanings.

INITIALS. Initials in people's names, or in companies named after them, take points (with a space between initials and name, but not between initials). Thus, **F.W. de Klerk, J.P. Morgan, A.E. Housman**. The only exceptions are for PEOPLE, COMPANIES and ORGANISATIONS that deliberately leave the points out. In general, follow the practice preferred by themselves in writing their own names. See also ABBREVIATIONS.

INTERNMENT. Generally considered a preferable penalty to **interment**: the former means **confinement**, the latter means **burial**.

INVESTIGATIONS of, not **into.**

ITALICS. Use italics for:

1. *Foreign words and phrases*
Foreign words and phrases, such as **cabinet** (French type), **chaebol, glasnost, intifada, Mitbestimmung, papabile, perestroika, ujamaa,** should be in italics. Remember to put on the appropriate accents and diacritical marks. Make sure that the meaning of any foreign word you use is clear. See also ACCENTS; ANIMALS, PLANTS, ETC; FOREIGN WORDS AND PHRASES; LATIN.

The following words and phrases are so familiar that they have become anglicised, so they should be in roman:

ad hoc
apartheid
a priori
a propos
avant-garde
bona fide
bourgeois
café
coup d'etat (but *coup de foudre*)
de facto, de jure
de rigeur
doppelganger(s)
elite
en masse, en route
in situ
machismo
nouveau riche
parvenu
pogrom
post mortem
putsch
raison d'etre
realpolitik
status quo
vice versa
vis-a-vis

2. *Newspapers and periodicals*

Note that only ***The Economist*** and ***The Times*** have **The** italicised. Thus the ***Daily Telegraph***, the ***New York Times***, the ***Observer***, the ***Spectator***, the ***Independent***, the ***Financial Times*** (but ***Le Monde, Die Welt, Die Zeit***). The ***Yomiuri Shimbun*** should be italicised; you can also say the ***Yomiuri*** or the ***Yomiuri*** newspaper, since ***shimbun*** simply means newspaper in Japanese. The ***Nikkei*** is an abbreviation (for ***Nikon Keizai***) and so should not be written as ***Nikkei Shimbun***.

3. *Books, pamphlets, plays, radio and television programmes*

These are roman, with capital letters for each main word, in quotation marks. Thus: **"Pride and Prejudice"**, **"Much Ado about Nothing"**, **"Any Questions"**, **"Crossfire"**, etc. But **the Bible** and its books (**Genesis, Ecclesiastes, John**, etc) do not have inverted commas.

However, book publishers generally use italics for books and pamphlets, plays, radio and television programmes.

4. *Lawsuits*

If abbreviated, ***versus*** should always be shortened to ***v***, with no point after it. Thus: **Brown *v* Board of Education, Coatsworth *v* Johnson.**

5. *The names of ships, aircraft, spacecraft*

Thus: HMS ***Illustrious, Spirit of St Louis, Challenger***, etc.

Note that a ship is **she**; a country is **it**.

J • K

Jargon. Avoid it. All sections of *The Economist* should be intelligible to all our readers, many of whom speak English only as a second language. You may have to think harder if you are not to use jargon, but you can still be precise. Technical terms should be used in their proper context only. In many instances simple words can do the job of **exponential** (try **fast**), **interface** (**frontier** or **border**), and so on. Avoid, above all, the kind of jargon that tries either to dignify nonsense with seriousness (**Working in an empowering environment**, a topic discussed at an Economist conference) or to obscure the truth (**We shall not launch the ground offensive until we have attrited the Republican Guard to the point when they no longer have an effective offensive capacity** – the Pentagon's way of saying that the allies would not fight on the ground until they had killed so many Iraqis that the others would not attack). What was meant by the Israeli defence ministry when it issued the following press release remains unclear: **The United States and Israel now possess the capability to conduct real-time simulations with man in the loop for full-scale theatre missile defence architectures for the Middle East.**

Just. If you can write **only** instead, do so.

•

Key. Keys may be **major** or **minor**, but not **low**. Few of the decisions, people, industries described as **key** are truly **indispensable**, and fewer still **open locks**.

L

Lag. If you **lag** transitively, you lag a pipe or a loft. Front-runners, rates of growth, fourth-quarter profits and so on **lag behind**.

Last. The last issue of *The Economist* implies our extinction; prefer **last week's** or the **latest** issue. Likewise avoid the **last** issue when referring to periodicals or journals: prefer the **latest**, **current**, **most recent** or (eg) **June** issue, or **this month's** or **last month's** issue.

Last year, in 2003, means 2002; if you mean the 12 months up to the time of writing, write **the past year**. The same goes for the **past** month, **past** week, **past** (not **last**) ten years. See also DATES.

Lifestyle. Prefer way of life.

Light-year. A light-year is a measurement of distance, not of time. It is the approximate distance travelled by light in one year.

Thus: 1 light-year = 5.88×10^{12} miles
9.46×10^{12} km

Like governs nouns and pronouns, not verbs and clauses. So **as in America** not **like in America**. But **authorities like Fowler and Gowers** is an acceptable alternative to **authorities such as Fowler and Gowers**.

Locate, in all its forms, can usually be replaced by something less ugly. **The missing scientist was located** means he was **found. The diplomats will meet at a secret location** means either that they will meet **in a secret place** or that they will meet **secretly. A company located in Texas** is simply **a company in Texas.**

Lower case. See CAPITALS.

M

MANILLA is a sort of envelope. **Manila** is the capital of the Philippines.

MASTERFUL means **imperious. Masterly** means **skilled.**

MAXIMISE means **to make as great as possible. Weight-lifting can maximise your biceps, but not your health.**

MAY and **might** are not always interchangeable, and you may want **may** more often than you think. If in doubt, try **may** first.

You need **might** in the past tense. **I may go to Leeds later** becomes, in the past, **I might have gone to Leeds later**. And in indirect past speech it becomes **I said I might go to Leeds later.**

Conditional sentences using the subjunctive also need **might**. Thus **If I were to go to Leeds, I might have to stand all the way.** This could be rephrased **If I go to Leeds, I may have to stand all the way.** Conditional sentences stating something contrary to fact, however, need **might: If pigs had wings, birds might raise their eyebrows.**

Do not write **George Bush might believe in education, but he thinks the people of Greece are Grecians.** It should be **George Bush may believe in education, but he thinks the people of Greece are Grecians.** Only if you are putting forward a hypothesis that may or may not be true are **may** and **might** interchangeable. Thus **If George Bush studies hard, he may (or might) learn the difference between Greek and Grecian.**

MEASUREMENTS. In most contexts that are not American or British, prefer **hectares** to **acres**, **kilometres** (or **km**) to **miles**, **metres** to **yards**, **litres** to **gallons**, **kilos** to **lb**, **tonnes** to **tons**, **Celsius** to **Fahrenheit**, etc. Regardless of which you choose, you should give an equivalent, on first use, in the other units: **It was hoped that after improvements to the engine the car would give 20km to the litre (47 miles per American gallon) compared with its present average of 15km per litre.**

Remember that in few countries do you now buy petrol in imperial gallons. In America it is sold in American gallons; in most places it is sold in litres.

See also MEASURES, pages 131ff.

MEDIA: prefer **press and television** or, if the context allows it, just

press. If you have to use the **media**, remember they are plural.

METAPHORS. "A newly invented metaphor assists thought by evoking a visual image," said George Orwell, "while on the other hand a metaphor which is technically 'dead' (eg, iron resolution) has in effect reverted to being an ordinary word and can generally be used without loss of vividness. But in between these two classes there is a huge dump of wornout metaphors which are merely used because they save people the trouble of inventing phrases for themselves."

Every issue of *The Economist* contains scores of metaphors:

a trail of crushed rivals
billing and cooing politicians
a smaller helping of Europe's manifest destiny
a project falling at the first hurdle
a weaker grip on monetary policy
a track record on inflation
tabloid reporters lapping up stories
a report leaving the door ajar
irresistible forces about to meet immovable objects
a roadblock in the path of reform
investors crying foul
a presidential U-turn
water off a duck's back in the Senate
a door slammed shut in China
a blind eye turned in Taiwan

Some of these are tired, and will therefore tire the reader. Most are so exhausted that they may be considered dead, and are therefore permissible. But use all metaphors, dead or alive, sparingly, otherwise you will make trouble for yourself.

An issue of *The Economist* chosen at random had a **package cutting the budget deficit, the administration loth to sign on to higher targets, liberals accused of playing politics on the court (Supreme, not tennis)**, only to find in the next sentence that **the boot was on the other foot, the lure of eastern Germany as a springboard to the struggling markets of Eastern Europe, West Europeanness helping to dilute an image**, someone **finding a pretext to stall the**

process before looking for **a few integrationist crumbs, a spring clean** that became in the next sentence **a stalking-horse for greater spending**, and **Michelin axing jobs in painful surgery** in order stay at **the top of a league table**. Soon the Michelin man **was plunging his company even further in to debt**, though if it were **to stay afloat his ambitions would have to be deflated**. The reader had to **go down to the seas again** two pages on when a **flotilla of mutual and quoted life-assurance outfits were confident of surviving turbulent waters. The galleons were afloat**, but **the medium-sized and smaller mutuals** quickly turned into **fodder for domestic and foreign predators**. Further on, **banks going to the altar in the expectation of a tax-free dowry** saw it become a **sweetener** in the next sentence and the bill that delivered it transformed into a **panacea**. Those who wanted to learn about Japanese equity financing were told of a **stockmarket crawling back** (not on its feet, it was explained) **towards its old high**, of **commercial banks keeping the wolf from the door** and, three paragraphs later, **of the stockmarket's double whammy**. On, on went the reader past **masked bunglings, key measures, money-supply growth out of hand, a haunted Bank of Japan redoubling its squeeze, banks slashing growth lest they found themselves on a tight leash before being cracked down on**. Few could have been surprised to learn at the end of the article that **another dose of higher interest rates might be forced on the banks if the present inflationary symptoms turned into measles-like spots, and if the apothecaries at the finance ministry agreed with the diagnosis**.

These two sentences, used as an opening paragraph to arrest the attention of the readers of *A.N. Other* newspaper, found their way past its subeditors and into print:

Bulgaria is on its knees. A long-simmering economic crisis has erupted, gripping the country in a fierce and unrelenting embrace.

Another publication believed:
If the panels were ever found, they might well reignite simmering tensions between Moscow and Berlin.

METE. You may **mete out** punishment, but if it is to fit the crime it is **meet.**

MILLIONAIRE. The time has gone when girls in the Bois du Boulogne would think that the term **millionaire** adequately described the man who broke the Bank at Monte Carlo. If you wish to use it, make it plain that **millionaire** refers to income (in dollars or pounds), not to capital. Otherwise try **plutocrat** or **rich man.**

MINIMISE means to make as small as possible; you cannot **slightly minimise** something.

MITIGATES mollifies, **militates** does the opposite.

MONOPOLY. A **monopolist** is the sole seller; a monopoly buyer is a **monopsonist.**

MOVE: do not use if you mean **decision, bid, deal** or something more precise. But **move** rather than **relocate.**

N

Names

Arab. Try to leave out the **al-**. If the name looks odd without it, include it (lower case, followed by hyphen). Names with **bin** also have no hyphen: **Osama bin Laden**, who becomes **Mr bin Laden** on subsequent mention. Use **Muhammad** unless it is part of the name of someone who spells it differently.

Bangladeshi, Pakistani. If the name includes the Islamic definite article (**ur** in Bangladeshi, **ul** in Pakistani), it should be lower case and without any hyphens: **Mujib ur Rahman**, **Zia ul Haq**, **Mahbub ul Haq**. **Sadruddin**, **Mohieddin** and **Saladin** are single words.

Chinese. In general follow the Pinyin spelling, which has replaced the old Wade-Giles system, except for people from the past, and people and places outside mainland China. **Peking** is therefore **Beijing** and **Mao** is **Zedong**, not **Tse-tung**.

There are no hyphens in Pinyin spelling. So:

	But
Deng Xiaoping	Chiang Kai-shek
Guangdong (Kwangtung)	Hong Kong
Guangzhou (Canton)	Li Ka-shing
Hu Jintao	Lee Teng-hui
Jiang Zemin	Tung Chee-Hwa
Mao Zedong (Tse-tung)	
Qingdao (Tsingtao)	
Tianjin (Tientsin)	
Xinjiang (Sinkiang)	
Zeng Qinghong	
Zhao Ziyang	
Zhu Rongji	

The family name in China comes first, so **Jiang Zemin** becomes **Mr Jiang** on a later mention.

Names from **Singapore**, **Korea**, **Vietnam** have no hyphens: **Lee Kuan Yew**, **Kim Jong Il**, **Ho Chi Minh**, **Tran Duc Luong**. Again, the family name comes first. (See also page 48.)

See also FOREIGN WORDS AND PHRASES; PEOPLE; TITLES.

Dutch. If using first name and surname together, **vans** and **dens** are lower case: **Dries van Agt** and **Joop den Uyl**. But without their first names they become **Mr Van Agt** and **Mr Den Uyl; Hans van der Broek** becomes **Mr Van der Broek.** These rules do not always apply to Dutch names in Belgium and South Africa: **Karel Van Miert**, for instance (as well as **Mr Van Miert**).

FRENCH. Any **de** is likely to be lower case, unless it starts a sentence. **De Gaulle** goes up; **Charles de Gaulle** goes down. So does **Yves-Thibault de Silguy.**

GERMAN. Any **von** is likely to be upper case only at the start of a sentence.

ITALIAN. Any **De** is likely to be upper case, but there are exceptions, so check.

JAPANESE. Although the Japanese put the family name first in their own language (Koizumi Junichiro), they generally reverse the order in western contexts. So we, too, refer to **Junichiro Koizumi.**

KOREAN. South Koreans have changed their convention to **Kim Dae-jung.** But north Koreans have stuck to **Kim Jong Il.** Kim is the family name.

RUSSIAN. Each of the different approaches to transliterating Russian has its drawbacks. The following rules of thumb are chosen chiefly for reasons of simplicity, not phonetic accuracy.

1. No y before e: **Belarus**, ***perestroika.*** Exception: if the e starts the word: **Yeltsin, Yevgeny.**

2. Where pronunciation demands it, use y before a at the start of a word, but not at the end: **Yavlinsky, Yakovlev, Alia** (not **Aliya**). But **Chechnya** and **Niyazov.**

3. Anything pronounced yo is usually spelled e: **Fedorov, Gorbachev.**

4. With words ending -ski, -skii or -sky, choose -sky. But with all other words ending -i, -ii or -y, choose -i. Thus **Zhirinovsky** and **Tchaikovsky**, but **Bolshoi, Rutskoi, Yuri.** Exceptions: **Grigory** (because of the association with Gregory) and **Nizhny Novgorod.**

5. Replace dzh with j. So: **Jokar, Jaba.**

Ukrainian. Ukrainians are engaging in retransliterating Russian versions of their words, often several times. It is impossible to keep up, so go for the familiar, if there is one. Ukrainian has no g, so it is **Yevhen** (not **Yevgeny**), **Ihor** (not **Igor**) and **Luhansk** (not **Lugansk**).

Negative. Use with care. A **negative** report is probably a **critical** report. It does not mean **bad**.

Neither ... nor. See NONE.

None usually takes a singular verb. So does **neither** (or **either**) **A nor** (or **or**) **B**, unless B is plural, as in **Neither the Dutchman nor the Danes have done it**, where the verb agrees with the element closest to it.

Nor means **and not**, so should not be preceded by **and**.

Not only. This should appear next to the item it qualifies. **His sister loved not only him** and **his sister not only loved him** have different meanings. When used with **but also**, it must either follow the verb or the verb must be repeated, eg, **he not only hurt her feelings but also hurt her pride**, better phrased as **he hurt not only her feelings but also her pride** (see the advice given under BOTH ... AND).

Numbers. See FIGURES, pages 29–30; MEASUREMENTS, page 43; MEASURES, pages 131ff.

O

One. Try to avoid **one** as a personal pronoun. **You** will often do instead.

Only. Put **only** as close as you can to the words it qualifies. Thus, **These animals mate only in June**. To say **They only mate in June** implies that in June they do nothing else. Always prefer **only** to **just**.

On to not **onto**.

Overseas. Increasingly used, and often wrongly, to mean **abroad** or **foreign**.

Overwhelm means **submerge utterly, crush, bring to sudden ruin**. Majority votes, for example, seldom do any of these things.

Oxymoron. An **oxymoron** is not an unintentional contradiction in terms but **a figure of speech in which contradictory terms are deliberately combined**, as in bitter-sweet, cruel kindness, sweet sorrow.

P

PEOPLE. Call them what they want to be called, short of festooning them with titles. Use full stops (points) after initials.

Here are some names which may present problems. See also FOREIGN WORDS AND PHRASES; NAMES; SPELLING; TITLES.

Heidar Aliev
Kofi Annan
Yasser Arafat
Bashir Assad
Omar Bashir
Zine el-Abidine Ben Ali
Ritt Bjerregaard
Frits Bolkestein
Boutros Boutros-Ghali
Zbigniew Brzezinski
Cuauhtémoc Cárdenas
Nicolae Ceausescu
Luiz Inácio Lula da Silva
Carlo De Benedetti
Carla Del Ponte
Yves-Thibault de Silguy
Carlo Ripa di Meana
Lawrence Eagleburger
Garret FitzGerald
Gandhi
Hans-Dietrich Genscher
Valéry Giscard d'Estaing
Felipe González
Mikhail Gorbachev
Gurkha
Jorg Haider
Elias Hrawi
Saddam Hussein
Radovan Karadzic
Muhammad Khatami
Ahmad Khomeini
Jeane Kirkpatrick
Junichiro Koizumi
Alexander Lukashenka
Slobodan Milosevic
François Mitterrand
Ratko Mladic
Mahathir Mohamad
King Mohammed of Morocco
Daniel arap Moi
Hosni Mubarak
Nursultan Nazarbaev
Benjamin Netanyahu
Saparmurat Niyazov

Gaafar Numeiri
Mullah Mohammed Omar
Velupillai Prabhakaran
Muammar Qaddafi
Ali Akbar Rafsanjani
Condoleezza Rice
Andrei Sakharov
Ali Abdullah Saleh
Wolfgang Schäuble
Gerhard Schröder
Yitzhak Shamir
Edward Shevardnadze
George Shultz
Mario Soares (Portugal)
Javier Solana
Alexander Solzhenitsyn
Adolfo Suárez (Spain)
Megawati Sukarnoputri
Aung San Suu Kyi
Jean Tiberi
Atal Behari Vajpayee
Abdurrahman Wahid
Caspar Weinberger
Vladimir Zhirinovsky
Gennady Zyuganov

PER CENT is not the same as a percentage point. A fall from 4% to 2% is a drop of 2 percentage points, or of 50%, but not of 2%. Nothing can fall, or be devalued, by more than 100%. If something trebles, it increases by 200%. See also FIGURES.

PERCOLATE means to pass **through**, not **up** or **down**.

PERSPICACITY and **perspicuity** should be the twin aims of writers: an acuteness of understanding coupled with lucidity of expression.

PHASE. When discussing incomes policies, monetary unions, extended plans, etc, prefer **stage** to **phase**.

PHONE: permissible, especially when preceded by **mobile**. But use sparingly, and generally prefer **telephone**.

PHOTO: not permissible, so use **photograph**.

PLACES. Use English forms when they are in common use: **Cologne**, **Leghorn**, **Lower Saxony**, **Lyons**, **Marseilles**, **Naples**, **Nuremberg**, **Turin**. And English rather than American – **Rockefeller Centre**, **Pearl Harbour** – unless the place name is part of a company name, such as **Rockefeller Center Properties Inc**. But follow local practice when a country expressly changes its name, or the names of rivers, towns, etc, within it. Thus **Almaty** not **Alma Ata**; **Chemnitz** not **Karl-Marx-Stadt**; **Chennai** not **Madras**; **Kolkata** not **Calcutta**; **Côte d'Ivoire** (and **Ivorians**) not **Ivory Coast**; **Mumbai** not **Bombay**; **Myanmar** not **Burma**; **Nizhny Novgorod** not **Gorky**; **St Petersburg** not **Leningrad**; and **Yangon** not **Rangoon**.

Zaire is now **Congo**. In contexts where there can be no confusion with the former French country of the same name, plain **Congo** will do. But call it **Congo-Kinshasa** if there is any risk of misunderstanding. The other Congo should always be **Congo-Brazzaville**. The river is now also the **Congo**. The people of either country are also **Congolese**.

Do not use the definite article before **Krajina**, **Lebanon**, **Piedmont**, **Punjab**, **Sudan**, **Transkei** and **Ukraine**, but it is **the Caucasus**, **the Gambia**, **The Hague**, **the Maghreb**, **the Netherlands** - and **La Paz**, **Le Havre**, **Los Angeles**. See also COUNTRIES AND THEIR INHABITANTS, pages 21–22, and STATES, ETC, pages 152ff.

Do not use the names of capital cities as synonyms for their governments. **Britain will send a gunboat** is fine, but **London will send a gunboat** suggests that this will be the action of the people of London alone. To write **Washington and Moscow now differ only in their approach to Havana** is absurd.

Although the place is **western** (or **eastern**) **Europe**, euphony dictates that the people are **west** or **east Europeans**.

Here are the spellings of some common problematic place names.

Abkhazia
Argentina (adj and people Argentine, not Argentinian)
Ashgabat
Azerbaijan
Baghdad
Bahamas, Bahamian
Bahrain
Bangladesh
Basel
Belarus
Beqaa
Bophuthatswana
Bosnia & Hercegovina
Bosporus
Britannia, Britannic
Brittany, Breton
Cameroon
Cape Town
Caribbean
Cincinnati
Colombia (South America)
Columbia (university, District of), British Columbia
Cracow
Dar es Salaam
Dhaka
Djibouti
Dominica (Caribbean island)
Dominican Republic (part of another island)
El Salvador, Salvadorean
Gettysburg
Gothenburg
Grozny
Gujarat, Gujarati
Guyana (but French Guiana)
Hanover
Harare
Hong Kong (the place)
Issyk-Kul
Jeddah
KaNgwane
Katmandu
Kazakhstan
Kirgizstan
Krajina
Kuwait city
KwaNdebele
KwaZulu-Natal
Luhansk
Luxembourg
Macau
Mafikeng
Mauritania
Middlesbrough
Mpumalanga (formerly Eastern Transvaal)

Nagorno-Karabakh
Nuremberg
Ouagadougou
Philippines (the people are Filipinos and Filipinas)
Phnom Penh
Pittsburgh
Putumayo
Pyrenees, Pyrenean
Reykjavik
Rheims
Romania
Rwanda, Rwandan
Salonika (not Thessaloniki)
São Paulo
Salzburg
Sindh
Srebrenica
Sri Lanka
Strasbourg
Suriname
Taipei
Tajikistan
Teesside
Tehran
Tigray, Tigrayan
Transdniestria
Uffizi
Uzbekistan
Valletta
Yangzi
Yugoslavia
Zepa
Zepce
Zurich

PLANE. This is a **tool**, a **surface** or, if it flies, an **aeroplane**, **aircraft** or **airliner** (not an **airplane**). **Warplane**, however, is allowed.

PLANTS. See ANIMALS, PLANTS, ETC.

PLURALS. No rules here. The spelling of the following plurals may be decided by either practice or derivation.

-a

addenda
bacteria
consortia
corpora (plural of corpus)
corrigenda
criteria
data
errata
genera (plural of genus)
media (the press, etc)
memoranda
phenomena
quanta
sanatoria
spectra
strata

-ae

amoebae
antennae
formulae
lacunae
nebulae
vertebrae

-eaus

bureaus (*but* bureaux de change)
plateaus
tableaus

-eaux

chateaux

-es

amanuenses
analyses
antitheses
bases
crises
hypotheses
oases
synopses

-i

alumni
fungi
nuclei
bacilli
genii
stimuli
cacti
graffiti
termini

-oes

archipelagoes
heroes
potatoes
buffaloes
innuendoes
salvoes
cargoes
mangoes
tomatoes
desperadoes
mementoes
tornadoes
dominoes
mosquitoes
torpedoes
echoes
mottoes
vetoes
embargoes
noes
volcanoes
haloes

-os

albinos
folios
placebos
armadillos
ghettos
provisos
commandos
impresarios
quangos
demos
librettos
radios
dynamos
major-domos
silos
embryos
manifestos
solos
Eskimos
memos
sopranos
falsettos
mulattos
stilettos
fandangos
oratorios
studios
fiascos
peccadillos
virtuosos
flamingos
pianos
weirdos

-s

agendas
milieus
quotas
arenas
panaceas

-ums

conundrums
moratoriums
stadiums
crematoriums
nostrums
symposiums
curriculums
quorums
ultimatums
forums
referendums
vacuums
mediums (spirit)

-uses

buses
fetuses
geniuses
caucuses
focuses
prospectuses
circuses

-ves	*-fs*
calves	dwarfs
halves	handkerchiefs
hooves	roofs
scarves	turfs
wharves	

Officials

attorneys-general	lords lieutenant	secretaries-general
field-marshals	major-generals	sergeant-majors
lieutenant-governors		

Indexes (of books); **indices** are indicators of index numbers.

Appendixes (anatomical variety); use **appendices** for the literary sort.

POSITIVE means **definitely laid down, beyond possibility or doubt, absolute, fully convinced** or **greater than zero.** It does not mean **good. It was a positive meeting** probably means **It was a good,** or **fruitful, meeting. Positive thoughts** mean **optimism.**

PRACTICABLE means **feasible. Practical** means **useful.**

PRECIPITOUS means **extremely steep**; a rash or hasty action is **precipitate. Precipitate share dealings led to a precipitous drop in prices.**

PREMIER, as a noun, should be confined to the first ministers of the Canadian provinces, German *Länder* and other sub-national states. Do not use it as a synonym for the prime minister of a country.

PREPOSITIONS at the end of sentences are permissible: **an example such as this is a good one to go by**, rather than **an example such as this is a good one by which to go.** But avoid **up to**, which can mean anything.

PRESENTLY means **soon**, not **at present. "Presently Kep opened the door of the shed, and let out Jemima Puddle-Duck."** (Beatrix Potter)

PRESSURISE. This is what you want in an aircraft, but not in an argument or encounter where persuasion is being employed. The verb you want here is **press** (use **pressure** only as a noun).

PREVARICATE means **evade the truth; procrastinate** means **delay.**

PRISTINE means **in its original** or **former condition**, not **pure** or **clean.**

PROACTIVE. Not a pretty word: try **active** or **energetic.**

PROBLEM. The problem with problem is it is overused, so much so that it is becoming a problem word.

PROCESS. A word properly applied to the Arab-Israeli peace affair, because it was meant to be evolutionary, but now often used in place of **talks.**

Proofreading

Look for errors in the following categories.

1. "Typos", which include misspelt words, punctuation mistakes, wrong numbers, transposed words or sentences.
2. Bad word breaks (see page 61).
3. Layout mistakes: wrongly positioned text (including captions, headings, folios, running heads) or illustrations, incorrect line spacing, missing items, widows (short lines at the top of a page).
4. Wrong fonts: errors in the use of italic, bold, etc.

If the text contains cross-references to numbered pages or illustrations, the proofreader is often responsible for inserting the correct reference at page proof stage, and for checking cross-references.

The most effective way of proof-reading is to read the text several times, each time with a different aim in mind, rather than attempting to carry out all checks in one go.

PROOFREADING MARKS are illustrated on the following pages. The intention of these marks is to identify, precisely and concisely, the nature of an error and the correction required. When corrections are extensive or complex, it is usually better to spell out in full the correct form of the text rather than leave the typesetter to puzzle over a string of hieroglyphs, however immaculately drawn and ordered. Mark all proof corrections clearly and write them in the margin.

INSTRUCTION	TEXTUAL MARK	MARGINAL MARK AND NOTES
Correction is concluded	None	/ Make after each correction
Leave unchanged	••••• under characters to remain	
Insert in text the matter indicated in the margin	(caret mark)	New matter followed by
Delete	/ through character(s) or through words	
Delete and close up	through character(s) or through characters, eg, ofr, characterter	
Close up – delete space		
Substitute character or substitute part of one or more words	through character / or through words	new character or new word(s)
Wrong font. Replace with correct font	Encircle character(s) to be changed	or w.f.
Set in or change to roman type	Encircle character(s) to be changed	Rom.
Set in or change to italic	under character(s) to be set or changed	

INSTRUCTION	TEXTUAL MARK	MARGINAL MARK AND NOTES
Set in or change to capital letters	≡ under character(s) to be set or changed	≡
Set in or change to small capital letters	= under character(s) to be set or changed	=
Set in or change to bold type	∿∿∿ under character(s) to be set or changed	∿∿∿ or bold
Set in or change to bold italic type	under character(s) to be set or changed	
Change capital letters to lower case letters	Encircle character(s) to be changed	≢ or l.c.
Change italic to upright type	Encircle character(s) to be changed	
Invert type	Encircle character to be changed	
Substitute or insert character in "superior" position	/ through character or ⋌ where required	under character eg
Substitute or insert full stop or decimal point	/ through character or ⋌ where required	⊙
Substitute or insert comma	/ through character or ⋌ where required	,

INSTRUCTION	TEXTUAL MARK	MARGINAL MARK AND NOTES
Substitute or insert colon	/ through character or ⋌ where required	(:)
Insert hyphen	/ through character or ⋌ where required	
Substitute or insert semi-colon	/ through character or ⋌ where required	;
Insert space	⋌ or /	
Equal space	between words or letters	
Reduce space	between words or letters	
Start new paragraph		
Run on (no new paragraph)		
Transpose characters or words	between characters or words, numbered when necessary	
Transpose lines		
Indent		
Move to the left	|←[xxxx]	
Insert single or double quotes	⋌ where required	

Proofreading (continued)

Word breaks. It may be necessary to break words, using a hyphen, at the end of lines. Computer word-processing programs come with standard hyphenation rules but these can always be changed or overruled. Ideally, the aim should be to make these breaks as undisruptive as possible, so that the reader does not stumble or falter. Whenever possible, the word should be broken so that, helped by the context, the reader can anticipate the whole word from the part of it given before the break. Here are some useful principles for deciding how to break a word.

1. Words that are already hyphenated should be broken at the hyphen, not given a second hyphen.
2. Words can be broken according to either their derivation (the British convention) or their pronunciation (the US convention): thus, **aristo-cracy** (UK) or **aristoc-racy** (US), **melli-fluous** (UK) or **mellif-luous** (US). See PART II for American usage.
3. Words of one syllable should not be broken.
4. Words of five or fewer characters should not be broken.
5. At least three characters must be taken over to the next line.
6. Words should not be broken so that their identity is confused or their identifying sound is distorted: thus, avoid **wo-men**, or **fo-ist**.
7. Personal names and acronyms (eg, NATO) should not be broken.
8. Figures should not be broken or separated from their unit of measurement.
9. A word formed with a prefix or suffix should be broken at that point: thus, **bi-furcated**, **ante-diluvian**, **convert-ible**.
10. If a breakable word contains a double consonant, split it at that point: thus, **as-sess**, **ship-ping**, **prob-lem**.
11. Do not hyphenate the last word on the right-hand page.

Propaganda (which is singular) means **a systematic effort to spread doctrine or opinions**. It is not a synonym for **lies**.

Proper nouns: if they have adjectives, use them. Thus a **Californian** (not **California**) **judge**, the **Pakistani** (not **Pakistan**) **government**, the **Texan** (not **Texas**) **press**.

Protest. By all means **protest your innocence** or **your intention to write good English**, if you are making a declaration. But if you are making a complaint or objection, you must **protest at** or **against** it.

Punctuation

APOSTROPHES. Use the normal possessive ending **'s** after singular words or names that end in **s**: **boss's, caucus's, Delors's, St James's, Jones's, Shanks's.** Use it after plurals that do not end in **s**: **children's, Frenchmen's, media's.**

Use the ending **s'** on plurals that end in **s** – **Danes', bosses', Joneses'** – including plural names that take a singular verb, eg, **Reuters', Barclays', Stewarts & Lloyds', Salomon Brothers'.**

Although singular in other respects, the United States, the United Nations, the Philippines, etc, have a plural possessive apostrophe: eg, **What will the United States' next move be?**

Peoples' = of peoples. **People's** = of (the) people.

Try to avoid using **Lloyd's** (the insurance market) as a possessive; it poses an insoluble problem.

The vulnerable part of the hero of the Trojan war is best described as an **Achilles** heel.

Do not put apostrophes into decades: the **1990s** not the **1990's.**

BRACKETS. If a whole sentence is within brackets, put the full stop inside.

Square brackets should be used for interpolations in direct quotations: **"Let them [the poor] eat cake."** To use ordinary curved brackets implies that the words inside them were part of the original text from which you are quoting.

COLONS. Use a colon "to deliver the goods that have been invoiced in the preceding words" (Fowler). **They brought presents: gold, frankincense and oil at $35 a barrel.**

Use a colon before a whole quoted sentence, but not before a quotation that begins mid-sentence. **She said: "It will never work." He retorted that it had "always worked before".**

Use a colon for antithesis or "gnomic contrasts" (Fowler). **Man proposes: God disposes.**

COMMAS. Use commas as an aid to understanding. Too many in one sentence can be confusing.

It is not necessary to put a comma after a short phrase at the start of a sentence if no natural pause exists there: **On August 2nd he invaded. Next time the world will be prepared.** But a breath, and so a comma, is needed after longer passages: **When it was plain that he had his eyes on Saudi Arabia as well as Kuwait, America responded.**

Use two commas, or none at all, when inserting a clause in the middle of a sentence. Thus, do not write: **Use two commas, or none at all when inserting …** or **Use two commas or none at all, when inserting …**

If the clause ends with a bracket, which is not uncommon (this one does), the bracket should be followed by a comma.

Do not put a comma before **and** at the end of a sequence of items unless one of the items includes another **and.** Thus **The doctor suggested an aspirin, half a grapefruit and a cup of broth.** But **He ordered scrambled eggs, whisky and soda, and a selection from the trolley.** But American usage is different; see PART II.

Commas can alter the sense of a sentence. To write **Mozart's 40th symphony, in G minor**, with commas indicates that this symphony was written in G minor. Without commas, **Mozart's 40th symphony in G minor** suggests he wrote 39 other symphonies in G minor.

Do not put commas after question marks, even when they would be separated by quotation marks: **"May I have a second helping?" he asked.**

Commas in dates: none.

DASHES. You can use dashes in pairs for parenthesis, but not more than one pair per sentence, ideally not more than one pair per paragraph. (See also HYPHENS.)

Use a dash to introduce an explanation, amplification, paraphrase, particularisation or correction of what immediately precedes it. Use it to gather up the subject of a long sentence, or to introduce a paradoxical or whimsical ending to sentences. Do not use the dash as a punctuation maid-of-all-work (Gowers).

FULL STOPS. Use plenty. They keep sentences short. This helps the reader.

Do not use full stops in ABBREVIATIONS or at the end of headings.

INVERTED COMMAS (QUOTATION MARKS). Use single ones only for quotations within quotations. Thus: **"When I say 'immediately', I mean some time before April," said the spokesman.**

When a quotation is indented and set in smaller type than the main text, do not put inverted commas around it.

For the relative placing of quotation marks and punctuation, follow the "Oxford Guide to Style" (formerly "Hart's Rules"). If an extract ends with a full stop or question-mark, put the punctuation before the closing inverted commas. **His maxim was that "love follows laughter." In this spirit came his opening gambit: "What's**

the difference between a buffalo and a bison?" If a complete sentence in quotes comes at the end of a longer sentence, the final stop should be inside the inverted commas. Thus, **The answer was, "You can't wash your hands in a buffalo." She replied, "Your jokes are execrable."**

If the quotation does not include any punctuation, the closing inverted commas should precede any punctuation marks that the sentence requires. Thus: **She had already noticed that the "young man" looked about as young as the New Testament is new. Although he had been described as "fawnlike in his energy and playfulness", "a stripling with all the vigour and freshness of youth", and even as "every woman's dream toyboy", he struck his companion-to-be as the kind of old man warned of by her mother as "not safe in taxis". Where, now that she needed him, was "Mr Right"?**

When a quotation is broken off and resumed after such words as **he said**, ask yourself whether it would naturally have had any punctuation at the point where it is broken off. If the answer is yes, a comma is placed within the quotation marks to represent this. Thus, **"If you'll let me see you home," he said, "I think I know where we can find a cab."** The comma after **home** belongs to the quotation and so comes within the inverted commas, as does the final full stop.

But if the words to be quoted are continuous, without punctuation at the point where they are broken, the comma should be outside the inverted commas. Thus, **"My bicycle", she assured him, "awaits me."**

See page 94 for American usage.

QUESTION-MARKS. Except in sentences that include a question in inverted commas, question-marks always come at the end of the sentence. Thus:

Where could he get a drink, he wondered?
Had Zimri peace, who slew his master?

SEMI-COLONS. Semi-colons should be used to mark a pause longer than a comma and shorter than a full stop. Don't overdo them.

Use them to distinguish phrases listed after a colon if commas will not do the job clearly. Thus, **They agreed on only three points: the ceasefire should be immediate; it should be internationally supervised, preferably by the OAU; and a peace conference should be held, either in Geneva or in Ouagadougou.**

Q • R

QUADRILLION. A thousand trillion.

•

RACISM. As a general rule, a person's race, colour or creed should be mentioned only when relevant. See also ETHNIC GROUPS.

REAL. Is it really necessary? When used to mean **after taking inflation into account**, it is legitimate. In other contexts (**Investors are showing real interest in the country, but Bolivians wonder if real prosperity will ever arrive**), it is often better left out.

REBUT means **repel** or **meet in argument. Refute**, which is stronger, means **disprove**. But neither of them is a synonym for **deny**. (**"Shakespeare never has six lines together without a fault. Perhaps you may find seven: but this does not refute my general assertion."** Samuel Johnson)

REGRETTABLY means it is to be regretted that; someone who shows regret is behaving **regretfully. It is regrettably true that few people respond regretfully when told they have dropped some litter.**

RELATIONSHIP is a long word often better replaced by **relations. The two countries hope for a better relationship** means **The two countries hope for better relations.**

RELATIVE: fine as an adjective, but as a noun prefer **relation**.

REPORT on, not **into**.

RESOURCES. Try to avoid, especially **human resources**, which may be **personnel, staff** or just **people.**

RING the bells, wring the hands.

RUN. In countries with a presidential system, you may **run** for office. In those with a parliamentary one, **stand.**

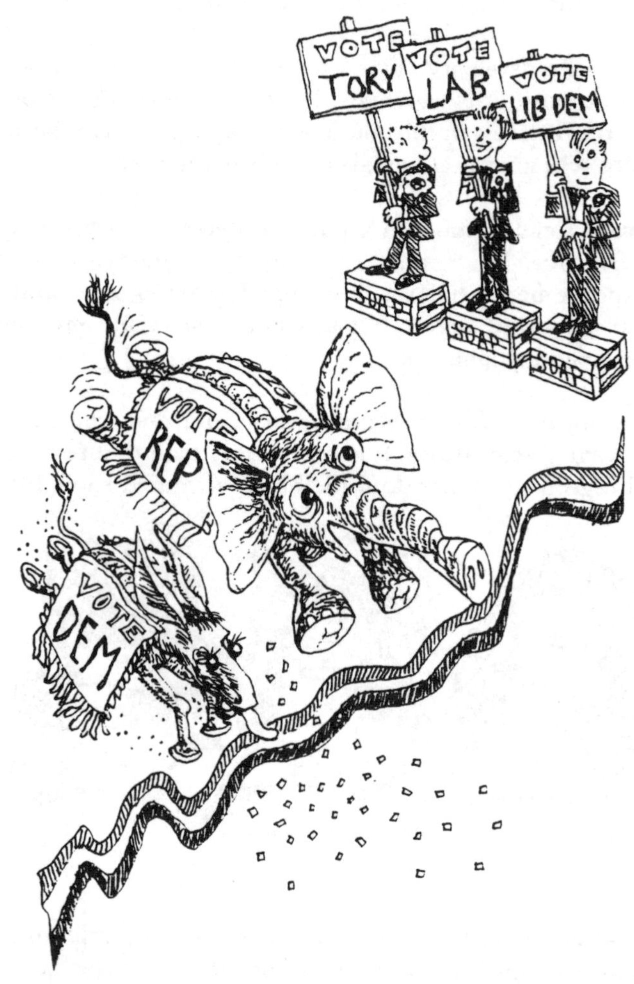

S

Same: often superfluous. If your sentence contains **on the same day that**, try **on the day that.**

Scotch. To **scotch** means to **disable**, not to **destroy**. (**"We have scotched the snake, not killed it"**). The people may be Scotch, Scots or Scottish (whisky is **Scotch**); choose as you like. **Scot-free** means **free from payment of a fine** (or **punishment**), not **free from Scotsmen.**

Sector: try **industry** instead or, for example, **banks** instead of **banking sector.**

Sensual means **carnal** or **voluptuous. Sensuous** means **pertaining to aesthetic appreciation,** without any implication of voluptuousness.

Sequestered means **secluded. Sequestrated** means **confiscated** or **made bankrupt.**

Sexism. It is often possible to phrase sentences so that they neither give offence to women nor become hideously complicated. Using the plural can be helpful. Thus **Instruct the reader without lecturing him** is better put as **Instruct the readers without lecturing them.** But some sentences cannot be satisfactorily rephrased in the plural: **Find a good teacher and take his advice** is not easily rendered gender-neutral. Avoid, above all, the sort of scrambled syntax that the Commission for Racial Equality had to adopt because it could not bring itself to use a singular pronoun: **We can't afford to squander anyone's talents, whatever colour their skin is.**

Avoid **chairperson** (chairwoman is permissible), **humankind** and **person in the street** – ugly expressions all. But remember that, in some contexts, the assumption that all people are men will be especially annoying just because it is wrong. **He will have to choose the best man for the job** is fine if you are talking about the pope selecting a bishop. If you are talking about Tony Blair appointing a new member of cabinet, it would be better to say **He will have to choose the best person for the job.**

Do not use words that make unwarranted assumptions about the sex of an interest-group and remember that gender may be unrelated to sex, even in English. Do you mean **housewives** or **consumers**, **mothers** or **parents**?

Refer to **women**, not **girls** (unless they are under 18) or **ladies. If more women read *The Economist*, there would be fewer jobs for the boys.**

SHORT WORDS. Use them. They are often Anglo-Saxon rather than Latin in origin. They are easy to spell and easy to understand. Thus prefer **about** to **approximately**, **after** to **following**, **let** to **permit**, **but** to **however**, **use** to **utilise**, **make** to **manufacture**, **plant** to **facility**, **take part** to **participate**, **set up** to **establish**, **enough** to **sufficient**, **show** to **demonstrate**, **before** to **prior to** and so on. **Underdeveloped** countries are often better described as **poor. Substantive** usually means **real** or **big.**

SIMON PURE is the **real person** (or thing), and has nothing to do with Caesar's wife or driven snow.

SIMPLISTIC: prefer **simple-minded, naive.**

SKILLS. These are turning up all over the place – in learning skills, thinking skills, teaching skills – instead of **the ability to ... He has the skills** probably means **He can.**

SLANG. Do not be too free with **slang** (eg, **He really hit the big time in 1999**). Slang, like metaphors, should be used only occasionally if it is to have effect. Avoid expressions used only by journalists, such as giving people **the thumbs up**, **the thumbs down** or **the green light**. Stay clear of **gravy trains** and **salami tactics**. Do not use **the likes of** or **set to** (as in **profits being set to rise**). And avoid words or expressions that are ugly or overused, such as **aggressive**, **the bot-**

tom line, high profile, caring (as an adjective), **carers, guesstimate** (use **guess**), **schizophrenic** (unless the context is medical), **crisis, hefty, key, major** (unless something else nearby is **minor**), **massive** (as in **massive inflation**), **meaningful, perceptions, prestigious, significant** and **tough.**

Politicians are often said to be highly **visible**, when **conspicuous** would be more appropriate. Regulations are sometimes said to be designed to create **transparency**, which presumably means openness. Elections described as **too close to call** are usually just **close.**

Try not to be predictable, especially not predictably jocular. Spare your readers any mention of **mandarins** when writing about the civil service, **players** when you are talking about businessmen or women and **their lordships** when discussing the House of Lords.

SMALL CAPITALS. Use small capitals for most abbreviations consisting of the first letter(s) of the abbreviated word(s). Exceptions are: currencies; degrees of temperature; some measures; and Latin numerals. See also ABBREVIATIONS.

SOI-DISANT means **self-styled**, not **so-called.**

SOME TIME means **at some point; sometime** means **former.**

SPECIFIC. A **specific** is a **medicine**, not a **detail.**

Spelling

Use British English rather than American English or any other kind (see also PART II). Sometimes, however, this injunction will clash with the rule that people and companies should be called what they want to be called, short of festooning themselves with titles. If it does, adopt American (or Canadian or other local) spelling when it is used in the name of an American (etc) company or private organisation (**Kaiser Aluminum, Pulverizing Services Inc, Travelers Insurance**), but not when it is being used for a place or government institution (**Pearl Harbour, Department of Defence, Department of Labour**). The principle behind this ruling is that place names are habitually changed from foreign languages into English: **Deutschland** becomes **Germany, München Munich, Torino Turin**, etc. And to respect the local spelling of government institutions would present difficulties: a sentence containing both the **Department of Labor** and the **secretary of labour**, or the **Defense Department** and the **need for a strong**

defence, would look unduly odd. That oddity will arise nonetheless if you have to explain that **Rockefeller Center Properties is in charge of Rockefeller Centre**, but with luck that will not happen too often.

The Australian **Labor Party** should be spelt without a **u** not only because it is not a government institution but also because the Australians spell it that way, although they spell **labour** as the British do.

Use **-ise, -isation (realise, organisation**, etc) throughout. **Apologise** or **apostrophise** but please do not **hospitalise**.

Follow the preferences of companies or individuals themselves in writing their names.

For spelling rules for place names, see COUNTRIES AND THEIR INHABITANTS; NAMES; PLACES; STATES, REGIONS, PROVINCES, COUNTIES.

For spelling rules for other proper names, see PEOPLE and COMPANIES.

Beware of computer program spell-checks.

Other common difficulties are listed below. See also -ABLE, -EABLE, -IBLE. See PART II for American spellings.

Common problems

abattoir
abut, abutted, abutting
accommodate
acknowledgment
acquittal
adrenalin
adviser, advisory
aeroplane, aircraft, airliner
aeon
aesthetic
aetiology
Afrikaans (the language), Afrikaner (the person)
ageing (*but* caging, paging, raging, waging)
agri-business
amiable
ambience
amok (*not* amuck)
analyse
annex (verb), annexe (noun)
appal, appals, appalling, appalled
aqueduct
arbitrager
artefact
asinine
balk (*not* baulk)
balloted, balloting
bandanna
bandwagon
battalion
benefited
biased
billeted
blanketing, blanketed
block (never bloc)
bogey (bogie is on a locomotive)
born (given birth to), borne (carried)
borsch
braggadocio
bused, busing (keep bussing for kissing)

by-election, bylaw, bypass, by-product, byword
bye (in sport only)
cannon (gun), canon (standard, criterion, clergyman)
canvas (cloth), canvass (seek opinion), canvassed
cappuccino
carcass
cash flow
caviar
chancy
channelled
checking account (spell it thus when explaining to Americans a current account, which is to be preferred)
choosy
cipher
clubable
combating, combated
commemorate
complement (make complete), compliment (praise)
connection
consensus
cooled, cooler, cooly
coral (stuff found in sea), corral (cattle pen)
cosseted, cosseting
council (assembly)
counsel (give advice)
defendant
dependant (person), dependent (adj)
depository (*unless* referring to American depositary receipts)
desiccation, desiccate
detente (*not* détente)
dexterous (*not* dextrous)
dignitary
dilapidate
discreet (prudent), discrete (separate)
disk (in a computer context), *otherwise* disc (including compact disc)
dispatch (*not* despatch)
dispel, dispelling
dissociate (*not* disassociate)
distil, distiller
divergences
douse (drench), dowse (use a divining rod)
doveish
dryer, dryly
dwelt
dyeing (colour)
dyke
embarrass (*but* harass)
encyclopedia
enroll, enrolment
ensure (make certain), insure (against risks)
enthrall
extrovert, introvert
farther (distance), further (additional)
ferreted
fetid
fetus (*not* foetus, misformed from the Latin *fetus*)
Filipino, Filipina (person), Philippine (adj of the Philippines)
filleted, filleting
flotation
flyer, high-flyer, frequent flyer
focused, focusing
forbear (abstain), forebear (ancestor)
forbid (past tense forbade)
foreboding
foreclose
forefather
forestall

forewarn
forgather
forgo (do without),
  forego (precede)
forsake
forswear, forsworn
fuelled
-ful, *not* -full (armful,
  bathful, handful, etc)
fulfil, fulfilling
fullness
fulsome
funnelling, funnelled
furore
glamour, glamorous
graffito, graffiti
gram (*not* gramme)
grey
grill (cook under flame)
grille (grating)
grisly (gruesome), grizzly (grey-
  haired; kind of bear)
guerrilla
gypsy
haemorrhage, haemorrhoids
haj
harass (*but* embarrass)
hiccup (*not* hiccough)
high-tech
Hizbullah
honour, honourable
hotch-potch
humour, humorous
idiosyncrasy
impostor
impresario
inadvertent
incur, incurring
innocuous
inoculate
inquire, inquiry (*not* enquire,
  enquiry except for official
  inquiries)
install, instalment, installation
instil, instilling
intransigent
jail (*not* gaol)
jewellery (*not* jewelry)
judgment
Koran
labelled, labelling
lacquer
laisser-faire
lama (priest), llama (beast)
lambast
leukaemia
levelling, levelled
liaise, liaison
libelled, libel (noun and verb)
licence (noun), license (verb)
lightening (making light),
  lightning (thunder and)
linchpin, lynch law
liquefy
liqueur (flavoured alcoholic
drink)
liquor (alcohol or other liquid)
literal (exact, factual, etc),
  littoral (shore)
loth (reluctant),
  loath (hate), loathsome
low-tech
manoeuvre (manoeuvring)
mantelpiece
marshal (noun and verb),
  marshalled
mayonnaise
medieval
meter (instrument for
  measuring),
  metre (linear measurement)
mileage
millennium (thousand years),
  millenarian (believer in the
  millennium)
minuscule

modelling, modelled
mould
mujahideen
Muslim (*not* Moslem)
naivety
nonplussed
nought (for numerals), *otherwise* naught
occur, occurring
optics, optician, ophthalmic, ophthalmology
paediatric (-ian)
panel, panelled
paraffin
parallel (-ed) paralleling
pastime
pedal (noun and verb, relating to foot lever)
peddle (to deal in trifles), *but* pedlar (not peddler)
peninsula (noun), peninsular (adj)
phoney (*not* phony)
piggyback (*not* pickaback)
plummeting, plummeted
Politburo
practice (noun), practise (verb)
predilection
preferred
preventive (*not* preventative)
pricey
principal (head; loan; or adj), principle (abstract noun)
privilege
proffered (-ing, *but* preferred)
profited
program (only in a computer context *otherwise* programme)
protester
Pushtu, Pushtun
pygmy
pzazz
questionnaire
queuing
rack (-ed, -ing, as in with pain, nerve-racking)
racket, *but* tennis racquet
rankle
rarefy
ratchet
raze (*not* rase)
razzmattazz
recur, recurrent, recurring
regretted, regretting
renege
repairable (able to be repaired), reparable (of loss, able to be made good)
resemble, resemblance
restaurateur
resuscitate
ropy
rottweiler
sacrilegious
salutary (remedial), salutatory (welcoming)
savannah
sceptic
seize
shaky
sheath (noun), sheathe (verb)
shenanigans
shibboleth
siege
sieve
skulduggery
smidgen (*not* smidgeon)
smoky
smooth (both noun and verb)
soothe
soyabean
specialty (*only* in context of medicine, steel and chemicals), *otherwise* speciality
sphinx

spoilt
stockmarket
storey (floor)
straitjacket, strait-laced, straight-faced
straits (narrow passage of water; position of difficulty)
stratagem
strategy
supersede
swap (*not* swop)
swathe
synonym
tariff
Tatar
teetotalism, teetotaller
threshold
titbits
titillate
tormentor
trade union, trade unions (*but* Trades Union Congress)
transatlantic, transpacific
transferred, transferring
transsexual
travelled, travelling
tricolor
trouper (as in old trouper)
tsar
tyre
unparalleled
untrammelled
vaccinate
vacillate
wagon (*not* waggon)
weasel, weaselly
wilful
withhold
wreath (noun), wreathe (verb)
wry, wrily
yogurt

Split infinitives. To never split an infinitive is quite easy.

Stationary: still. **Stationery**: writing paper, envelopes and so on.

Straight means **direct** or **uncurved**; **strait** means **narrow** or **tight**.

-style. Avoid **German-style supervisory boards**, **an EU-style rotating presidency**, etc. Explain what you mean.

Subcontract. If you engage someone to do something, you are **contracting** the job to him; only if he then asks someone else to do it is the job **subcontracted**.

Subjunctives. See INTRODUCTION, page 3; MAY AND MIGHT.

Supportive. Try **helpful** instead.

Systemic, systematic. The former means **relating to a system or body as a whole**. The latter means **according to system, methodical** or **intentional**.

T

TABLE: avoid it as a transitive verb. In Britain to **table** means to bring something forward for action. In America, however, it means exactly the opposite.

TARGET is a noun, as is **trial.** If you are tempted to use **target** as a verb, try **aim** or **direct. Targeted** means **provided with a shield.**

TESTAMENT is a will, **testimony** evidence. **It is testimony to the poor teaching of English that journalists habitually write testament instead.**

THERE IS, THERE ARE: often unnecessary. **There were smiles on every face** is better as **A smile was on every face. There are three issues facing the prime minister** is better as **Three issues face the prime minister.**

TIMES: take care. **Three times more than x** means **four times as much as x.**

TITLES.

The overriding principle is to treat people with respect. That usually means giving them the title they themselves adopt. But some titles are misleading (all Italian graduates are Dr), and some tiresomely long (Mr Dr Dr Federal Sanitary-Inspector Schmidt). Do not indulge people's self-importance unless it would seem insulting not to.

Do not use Mr, Mrs, Miss, Ms or Dr on first mention even in body-matter. Plain **George Bush, Tony Blair** or other appropriate combination of first name and surname will do. But thereafter for all living people drop the forename and use Mr, Mrs, Ms, Miss or some other title with the surname: **Jacques Chirac,** then **Mr Chirac. Governor**

X, President Y, the Rev John Z may be **Mr, Mrs** or **Miss** on second mention. Knights, dames, lords, princes, kings, etc, should be given their title on first and subsequent mentions. Those peers who are better known by their old names, like Paddy Ashdown or Margaret Thatcher, can be given their familiar names on first mention (only).

Avoid the habit of joining office and name: **Prime Minister Blair, Budget Commissioner Liikanen**; but **Chancellor Schröder** is permissible.

If you use a title, get it right. **Rear-Admiral** Jones should not, at least on first mention, be called **Admiral** Jones. Some titles serve as names, and therefore have initial capitals, though they also serve as descriptions: **the Archbishop of Canterbury, the Emir of Kuwait.** If you want to describe the office rather than the individual, use lower case: **The next archbishop of Canterbury will be a woman.** Use lower case, too, in references simply to **the duke, the emir, the shah: The Duchess of Scunthorpe was in her finery, but the duke wore jeans.**

1. *Headings and captions*

Titles are not necessary in headings or captions (surnames are; no Johns, Kens, Tonys, Newts, etc). Sometimes they can also be dispensed with for athletes and rock stars, if titles would make them seem more ridiculous than dignified.

2. *The dead*

No titles for the dead, except those whom you are writing about because they have just died. **Dr Johnson** and **Mr Gladstone** are also permissible.

3. *Foreign titles*

Take care with foreign titles. Malaysian ones are so confusing that it may be wise to dispense with them altogether. Do not, however, call **Tunku Razaleigh Hamzah** Mr Razaleigh Hamzah; if you are not giving him his Tunku, refer to him, on each mention, as **Razaleigh Hamzah**. Avoid, above all, Mr Tunku Razaleigh Hamzah.

4. *Medical and academic*

Use **Dr** only for qualified medical people, unless the correct alternative is not known or it would seem perverse to use **Mr**. And try to keep **Professor** for those who hold chairs, not just a university job or an inflated ego.

5. Life peeresses

Life peeresses should be called **Lady**, not **Baroness**, just as barons are called **Lord**.

6. Nicknames

Avoid nicknames and diminutives unless the person is always known (or prefers to be known) by one: **Tony Blair**, **Dick Cheney**, **Bill Emmott**, **Newt Gingrich**, **Tiny Rowland**.

7. Middle initials

Omit middle initials. You may have to distinguish between **George Bush junior** and **George Bush senior**, but nobody will imagine that the **Lyndon Johnson** you are writing about is **Lyndon A. Johnson** or **Lyndon C. Johnson**.

8. Ms

The title **Ms**, which was created to provide a female equivalent for the all-purpose male title Mr, is permissible though ugly. Married women who are known by their maiden names – eg, **Aung San Suu Kyi**, **Benazir Bhutto**, **Jane Fonda** – are **Miss** unless they have made it clear that they want to be called something else.

TO OR AND? To try and end the killing does not mean the same as **to try to end the killing**.

TOTAL: all right as a noun, but as a verb prefer **amount to** or **add up to**.

TRANSPARENCY. Try **openness** instead.

TRANSPIRE means **exhale**, not **happen**, **occur** or **turn out**.

TRILLION: a thousand billion (abbreviation trn). See also FIGURES, NUMBERS.

U

UNDERPRIVILEGED. Since a privilege is a special favour or advantage, it is by definition not something to which everyone is entitled. So **underprivileged**, by implying the right to privileges for all, is not just ugly jargon but also nonsense.

UNIQUE means **the only one of its kind** and cannot be qualified; it is nonsense to describe something as **almost/rather/the most unique**.

UNLIKE should not be followed by **in**. See LIKE.

UNNECESSARY WORDS. Some words add nothing but length to your prose. Use adjectives to make your meaning more precise and be cautious of those you find yourself using to make it more emphatic. The word **very** is a case in point. If it occurs in a sentence you have written, try leaving it out. **The omens were good** may have more force than **The omens were very good.**

Avoid **strike action (strike** will do), **cutbacks (cuts)**, **track record (record)**, **wilderness area** (usually either a **wilderness** or a **wild area)**, **large-scale (big)**, the **policymaking process (policymaking)**, **weather conditions (weather)**, etc. **This time around** just means **This time.**

Shoot off, or rather shoot, as many prepositions after verbs as possible. Thus people can **meet** rather than **meet with**; companies can be **bought** and **sold** rather than **bought up** and **sold off**; budgets can be **cut** rather than **cut back**; plots can be **hatched** but not **hatched up**; organisations should be **headed** by rather than **headed up** by chairmen just as markets should be **freed**, rather than **freed up**. And children can be **sent** to bed rather than **sent off** to bed. Also beware of overdoing the prefix **re-**. **Shuffle** and **supply** are better than **reshuffle** and **resupply**.

The word **community** is usually unnecessary. So the **black community** means **blacks**, the **business community** means **business**, the **homosexual community** means **homosexuals**, the **intelligence community** means **spies**, the **international community**, if it means anything, means **other countries**, **aid agencies** or, just occasionally, **the family of nations**.

Use words with care. A **heart condition** is usually a **bad heart**. A **near miss** is probably a **near hit**. **Positive thoughts** presumably means **optimism**, just as a **negative report** is probably a **critical report**. **Industrial action** is usually **industrial inaction**, **industrial disruption** or **strike**. A **substantially finished** bridge is an **unfinished** bridge, a **major speech** usually just a **speech**. Something with **reliability problems** probably **does not work**. If yours is a **live audience**, what would a dead one be like?

Certain words are often redundant. The leader of the **so-called** Front for a Free Freedonia is the leader of the Front for a Free Freedonia. A **top politician** or **top priority** is usually just a **politician** or a **priority**, and a **major speech** is usually just a speech. A **safe haven** is a **haven**. **Most probably** and **most especially** are **probably** and **especially**. **The fact that** can often be shortened to **That**. **That I did not do so was a self-indulgence.** **Loans to agricultural and industrial sectors** are just **loans to agriculture and farming**.

And the verb **tend to** adds no meaning to a sentence, being a fruitless way of either qualifying or adding emphasis. **The weather tends to be hot** really means **The weather is hot**.

USE AND ABUSE: two words much used and abused. You **take** drugs, not **use** them (Does he use sugar?). And **drug abuse** is just **drug taking**, as is **substance abuse**, unless it is **glue sniffing** or **bun throwing**.

V • W

VENAL. In some countries, petty officials are **venal** – that is, open to bribery. But, when you consider how little they are paid, you may count it a **venial** – that is, pardonable – sin.

VENERABLE means **worthy of reverence.** It is not a synonym for **old.**

VENUES: avoid them. Try **places.**

VERBAL. Every agreement, except the nod-and-wink variety, is **verbal.** If you mean one that was not written down, describe it as **oral.**

VIABLE means **capable of living.** Do not apply it to things like railway lines. **Economically viable** means **profitable.**

•

WARN is transitive, so you must either **give warning** or **warn somebody.**

WHEREABOUTS are plural.

WHICH informs, **that** defines. **This is the house that Jack built.** But **This house, which Jack built, is now falling down.**

WHILE (do not use **whilst**) is best used temporally. Do not use it in place of **although** or **whereas.**

WORLD WARS. Write **the second world war** or **the 1939–45 war**, not **world war two, II** or **2.** Similarly, prefer **the first world war** to **world war one, I** or **1. Post-war** and **pre-war** are hyphenated.

Generally the full names of **wars** should be lower case: **Crimean war, cold war, Gulf war.** But where this might be confusing, initial letters should be capitalised: **Wars of the Roses**, the **War of Independence**, the **Thirty Years' War.**

PART II

AMERICAN AND BRITISH ENGLISH

The differences between English as written and spoken in America and English as used in Britain are considerable, as is the potential for misunderstanding, even offence, when using words or phrases that are unfamiliar or mean something else on the other side of the Atlantic. This section highlights the important differences of American and British English spelling, grammar and usage.

Vocabulary. Sometimes the same word has taken on different meanings on the two sides of the Atlantic, creating an opportunity for misunderstanding. The word **homely**, for example, means **simple** or **informal** in British English, but **plain** or **unattractive** in American English.

This also applies to figures of speech. **It went like a bomb** in British English means it was a great success; **it bombed** in American English means it was a disaster. **To table** something in British English means to bring it forward for action; but in American English it means the opposite.

Exclusivity. What is familiar in one culture may be entirely alien in another. British English exploits terms and phrases borrowed from the game of cricket; American English uses baseball terms. Anyone writing for readers in both markets uses either set of terms at his peril. Do not make references or assumptions that are geographically exclusive, for example by specifying months when referring to seasonal patterns, by using north or south to imply a type of climate, or by making geographical references that give a state's name followed by USA, as in Wyoming, USA.

One writer's slang is another's lively use of words; formal language to one is pomposity to another. This is the trickiest area to negotiate when writing for both British and American readers. At its best, distinctively American English is more direct and vivid than its British English equivalent. Many American words and expressions have passed into British English because they are shorter or more to the point: phrases like **lay off**, preferable to **make redundant**. But American English also has a contrary tendency to lengthen words, creating a (to British readers) pompous tone: for instance, **transportation** (in British English, **transport**).

British English is slower than American English to accept new words, and suspicious of short cuts and sometimes it resists the use as verbs of nouns such as **author**, **critique**, **host**, **impact**, **haemorrhage**, **loan**, **party**, **pressure** and **roundtable**.

Syntax and sentence structure. American English may also use different syntax and sentence construction. Written American English tends to be more declarative than its British counterpart, and adverbs and some modifying phrases are frequently positioned differently. For example, British English may say, **"As well as going shopping, we went to the park."** American English would turn the opening phrase around: **"We went to the park as well as going shopping"**, or would begin the sentence with **"In addition to"**. British English also tends to use more compound modifying phrases, while American English prefers to go with simpler sentence structure.

In British English doctors and lawyers are to be found **in** Harley Street or Wall Street, not **on** it. And they rest from their labours **at** weekends, not **on** them. During the week their children are **at** school, not **in** it.

Words may also be inserted or omitted in some standard phrases. British English goes **to hospital**, American English **to the hospital**. British English chooses between **one or other thing**; American English chooses **one thing or the other**.

Spelling. Some words are spelt differently; the spellings are sufficiently similar to identify the word, but the unfamiliar form may still disturb the reader. It may be better to use a synonym than to take this risk, although sometimes it cannot be avoided.

Special problems. A number of subjects call for highly detailed, specialised guidance beyond the scope of this book, though some of the vocabulary is dealt with here. These areas include food and cookery (different names for ingredients and equipment; different systems of measurement); medicine and health care (different professional titles, drug names, therapies); human anatomy (different attitudes to the depiction of sexual organs); and gardening (different seasons and plants). Many crafts and hobbies also use different terms for equipment, materials and techniques.

Race and sex. The difficulties that arise in Europe with references to race and sex (see ETHNIC GROUPS, SEXISM) are even greater in America. When referring to Americans whose ancestors came from Africa, many people use **African-American** rather than **black**. It is unacceptable to refer to **American Indians** as **red**; they are often called **Native Americans.** It can also cause offence to describe the original inhabitants of the lands stretching from Greenland to Alaska as **Eskimos**; this was a corruption of a Cree word meaning **raw flesh eater**. The people themselves have at least three major tribal groupings. **Alaska natives** are usually called **native Americans** in Alaska. **Inuit** should be used only to refer to people from that tribe.

It is unwise to describe an adult American female as a **girl**.

A joint dictionary

Use -ize, not -ise. The American convention is to spell with **z** many words that some British writers (including *The Economist*) spell with **s**. Few British readers object to this. Remember, though, that some words must end in **-ise**, whichever spelling convention is being followed. These include:

advertise	despise	incise
advise	devise	merchandise
apprise	disguise	premise
arise	emprise	prise
chastise	enfranchise	revise
circumcise	excise	supervise
comprise	exercise	surmise
compromise	franchise	surprise
demise	improvise	televise

Note that words with the ending **-lyse**, such as **analyse** and **paralyse**, should not be spelt **-lyze** in British English, even though they are commonly spelt thus in American English.

Words generally acceptable in both British and American English.

ambience *not* ambiance
among *not* amongst
annex *not* annexe
artifact *not* artefact
backward *not* backwards
baptistry *not* baptistery
Bible (Scriptures), *not* bible
Bordeaux *not* claret, for red wine of region
burned *not* burnt
bus *not* coach
busy *not* engaged, for telephones
canvases *not* canvasses
car rental *not* car hire
cater to *not* cater for
custom-made *not* bespoke
day nursery *not* crèche
development *not* estate, for housing
diesel fuel *not* derv
disc *not* disk, except in computing
dispatch *not* despatch
encyclopedia *not* encyclopaedia
except for *not* save
farther *not* further, for distance
first name *not* Christian name
flashlight *not* torch
flip *not* toss, for coin, etc
focusing, focused, etc

fuel *not* petrol (UK) or gasoline (US)
forward *not* forwards
(eye)glasses *not* spectacles
grille *not* grill, for grating
gypsy *not* gipsy
hairdryer *not* hairdrier
horse-racing *not just* racing
inquire *not* enquire
insurance coverage *not* insurance cover
intermission *not* interval
jail *not* gaol
learned *not* learnt
like *not* fancy
line *not* queue
located *not* situated
location *not* situation
maid *not* chambermaid
mathematics *not* maths (UK) or math (US)
motorcycle *not* motorbike
neat *not* spruce or tidy
newsstand *not* kiosk
nightgown *not* nightdress
onto *not* on to
orangeade/lemonade *not* orange/lemon squash
overnight bag *not* holdall
package *not* parcel
parking spaces/garage *not* car park (UK) or parking lot (US)
phoney *not* phony
refrigerator *not* fridge
railway station *not* railroad station
raincoat *not* mac, mackintosh
rent *not* hire, except for people
reservation, reserve (seats, etc) *not* booking, book
retired person *not* old-age pensioner (UK) or retiree (US)
slowdown *not* go-slow, in production
soccer *not* football, except for American football
spelled *not* spelt
spoiled *not* spoilt
street musician *not* busker
swap *not* swop
swimming *not* bathing
team *not* side, in sport
tearoom *not* teashop
thread *not* cotton
toilet *not* lavatory
toll-free *not* free of charge
tuna *not* tunny
underwear *not* pants or knickers, or use lingerie for women's underwear
unmistakable *not* unmistakeable
unspoiled *not* unspoilt
while *not* whilst
whimsy, whimsies *not* whimsey, whimseys
workman *not* navvy
yogurt *not* yoghourt or yoghurt

Problematic words and phrases

DIFFERENT SPELLING CONVENTIONS.

American English is more obviously phonetic than British English. The word **cosy** becomes **cozy**, **aesthetic** becomes **esthetic**, **sizeable** becomes **sizable**, **arbour** becomes **arbor**, **theatre** becomes **theater**, **draught** becomes **draft**.

The main spelling differences between American English and British English are as follows.

-eable/-able. The silent **e**, created when forming some adjectives with this suffix, is more often omitted in American English; thus, **likeable** is spelt **likable**, **unshakeable** is spelt **unshakable**. But the **e** is sometimes retained in American English where it affects the sound of the preceding consonant; thus, **traceable**, or **manageable**.

-ae/-oe. Although it is now common in British English to write **medieval** rather than **mediaeval**, other words – often scientific terms such as **aeon**, **diarrhoea**, **anaesthetic**, **gynaecology**, **homoeopathy** – retain their classical composite vowel. In American English, the composite vowel is replaced by a single **e**; thus, **eon**, **diarrhea**, **anesthetic**, **gynecology**, **homeopathy**.

-ce/-se. In British English, the verb that relates to a noun ending in **-ce** is sometimes given the ending **-se**; thus, **advice** (noun), **advise** (verb), **device/devise**, **licence/license**, **practice/practise**. In the first two instances, the spelling change is accompanied by a slight change in the sound of the word; but in the other two instances, noun and verb are pronounced the same way, and American English spelling reflects this, by using the same spelling: thus, **license** and **practice**. It also extends the use of **-se** to other nouns which in British English are spelt **-ce**: thus, **defense**, **offense**, **pretense**.

-e/-ue. The final silent **e** or **ue** of several words is omitted in American English but retained in British English: thus, **analog/ analogue**, **ax/axe**, **catalog/catalogue**.

-ll/-l. In British English, when words ending in the consonant **l** are given a suffix beginning with a vowel (eg, the suffixes **-able**, **-ed**, **-ing**, **-ous**, **-y**), the **l** is doubled; thus, **annul/annulled**, **model/modelling**, **quarrel/quarrelling**, **rebel/rebellious**, **wool/woolly**. This is inconsistent with the general rule in British English that the final consonant is doubled before the suffix only when the preceding vowel carries the main stress: thus, the word **regret** becomes **regretted**, or **regrettable**; but the word **billet** becomes **billeted**. American English mostly does not have this inconsistency. So if the stress does not fall on the preceding vowel, the **l** is not doubled: thus, **model/modeling**, **travel/traveler**; but **annul/annulled**.

Several words which end in a single **l** in British English – eg, **appal**, **fulfil** – take a double **ll** in American English. In British English, the **l** stays single when the word takes a suffix beginning with a consonant (eg, the suffixes **-ful**, **-fully**, **-ment**): thus, **fulfil/ fulfilment**. Moreover, words ending in **-ll** usually lose one **l** when taking one of these suffixes: thus, **skill/skilful**, **will/wilfully**. In American English, words ending in **-ll** usually remain intact, whatever the suffix: thus, **skill/skillful**, **will/willfully**.

-our/-or. Most British English words ending in **-our** – **ardour**, **behaviour**, **candour**, **demeanour**, **favour**, **valour** and the like – lose the **u** in American English: thus, **ardor**, **candor**, etc. The major exception is **glamour**, which retains its **u**.

-re/-er. Most British English words ending in **-re** – such as **centre**, **fibre**, **metre**, **theatre** – end in **-er** in American English: thus, **center**, **fiber**, etc. Exceptions include: **acre**, **cadre**, **lucre**, **massacre**, **mediocre**, **ogre**.

-t/-ed (past tense). British English uses **-t** – **spelt**, **learnt**, **burnt** – whereas American English uses **-ed** – **spelled**, **learned**, **burned**.

Hyphenation.

American English is far readier than British English to accept compound words. In particular, many nouns made of two separate nouns are spelt as one word in American English, while in British English they would either remain separate or be joined by a hyphen: eg, **applesauce** (hyphenated in British English). British English also tends, more than American English, to use hyphens as pronunciation aids or to separate identical letters in words such as **co-operation**, **pre-empt**, **re-examine**.

Common problematic words.

The following list draws attention to commonly used words and idioms that either are spelt differently or have different meanings in American English and British English. It does not cover slang or colloquialisms.

If you want to produce a single version of written material which will be acceptable to both sorts of readers, you should avoid using the words in this list when there is a mutually acceptable alternative (see pages 84–85). If not, follow one or other convention, and, if this means using a word that will mystify or mislead one group of readers, provide a translation.

British	***American***
accommodation (lodging/s)	accommodation/s (lodging/s)
adopt (a candidate)	nominate
aerial (TV)	antenna
aluminium	aluminum
anti-clockwise	counterclockwise
apophthegm	apothegm
apple purée	applesauce
at weekends	on weekends
aubergine	eggplant
autumn	fall
baby's dummy	pacifier
baking tray	baking sheet
bag, handbag	purse, pocketbook
banknote	bill
barrister	trial lawyer
behove	behoove
bicarbonate of soda	baking soda
bill	check
biscuit (sweet)	cookie
biscuit (savoury)	cracker
black treacle	molasses
bowler (hat)	derby
braces	suspenders
building society	savings and loan association
cake tin	cake pan
calibre	caliber
camp bed	cot
car, saloon	sedan
car bonnet	hood
car boot	trunk
car demister	defogger
car jump leads	jumper cables
car park	parking lot
car silencer	muffler
car windscreen	windshield

British	*American*
car wing	fender
caravan	trailer
cheque (bank)	check
chequered	checkered (pattern)
chickpea	garbanzo bean (and chickpea)
chilli/chillies	chile/chiles, chili powder, chili con carne
chips	French fries
cinema	movie theater
clerk (bank)	teller
clever	smart
cling film	plastic wrap
coach	bus
cooker	stove
corn	wheat
cornflour	cornstarch
cosy	cozy
cot	crib
courgette	zucchini
crayfish	crawfish
crisps	potato chips
crossroads/junction	intersection
crystallised	candied
clothes cupboard/wardrobe	closet
desiccated coconut	shredded coconut
dialled	dialed
diary (appointments)	calendar
diary (record)	journal
digestive biscuit	graham cracker
district	neighborhood
dived	dove
double cream	heavy cream
draught	draft
dressing gown	bathrobe/housecoat/robe
dual carriageway	four-lane (or divided) highway
dyke	dike
essence (eg, vanilla)	extract or flavoring
estate agent	realtor/real estate agent
ex-serviceman	veteran
eyrie	aerie
film	movie
flan tin	pie plate

British	***American***
flat	apartment
fillet (boneless meat/fish)	filet
flour, plain	flour, all-purpose
flour, self-raising	flour, self-rising
flour, wholemeal	flour, whole-wheat
flyover	overpass
from ... to ...	through
frying pan	skillet (or frying pan)
fuelled	fueled
full stop (punctuation)	period
furore	furor
give way	yield
golden syrup	corn syrup
greengrocer's	vegetable store
grey	gray
grill (verb and noun)	broil (verb), broiler (noun)
ground floor	first floor
high street	main street
hire (of car)	rent or hire
holiday	vacation (*but* public holiday)
home from home	home away from home
homely	homey/homy (homely = plain)
icing sugar	powdered or confectioners' sugar
in (Fifth Avenue, etc)	on
increase (of money)	hike
jeweller/jewellery	jeweler/jewelry
jumper	sweater
kerb/kerbside	curb/curbside
labelled	labeled
ladder (in stocking)	run
lawyer	attorney (or lawyer)
lease of life	lease on life
lent	loaned
lift	elevator
liquidiser	blender
lorry	truck
lustre	luster
maize/sweetcorn	corn
manoeuvre/manoeuvrable	maneuver/maneuverable
mean (parsimonious)	stingy, tight (mean = nasty)
meet	meet with
metre (unit of distance)	meter

British	***American***
minced meat	ground meat
modelled	modeled
motor-racing	auto-racing
motorway	highway, freeway, expressway, throughway
mould/moulder/moult	mold/molder/molt
moustache	mustache
mum/mummy	mom/mommy
muslin	cheesecloth
nappy	diaper
nervy	nervous (nervy = brazen)
oblige	obligate
omelette	omelet
ordinary	regular, normal
outside	outside of
paddling pool	wading pool
panelled	wood-paneled
pants	underpants
pastry case	pie crust
pavement	sidewalk
pepper (red, green, etc)	sweet pepper or bell pepper
petrol	gasoline, gas
petrol station	gas/service station
pips	seeds (in fruit)
pitta bread	pita bread
plain/dark chocolate	semisweet or unsweetened chocolate
plait	braid
plough	plow
podgy	pudgy
polythene	polyethylene
post, post box	mail, mailbox
power point	electrical outlet
pram, push chair	baby buggy/carriage, stroller
programme (except computer)	program
property (land)	real estate
pyjamas	pajamas
quarters (three-quarters)	fourths (three-fourths)
queue	line, line up
quitted (past tense and participle of quit)	quit

British	***American***
rambler	hiker
rationalisation (personnel)	downsizing
removal van	moving van
removers	movers
riding (horses)	horseback riding
ring road	beltway
rivalled	rivaled
rocket (salad)	arugula
rowing boat	rowboat
rumbustious	rambunctious
scallywag	scalawag
sceptical	skeptical
senior	ranking (political)
shortcrust pastry	short pastry/basic pie dough
single cream	light cream
sizeable	sizable
skilful	skillful
sleepers	railroad ties
smoulder	smolder
solicitor	attorney, lawyer
sombre	somber
soya	soy
spanner	wrench
specialist shop	specialty shop
speciality (*but* specialty for medicine, steel and chemicals)	specialty
sponge finger biscuits	ladyfingers
spring onion	scallion
spring roll	egg roll
stand (for election)	run
starter	appetizer
stocks	inventory
stoned (cherries, etc)	pitted
storey (of building)	story, floor
stupid	dumb
subway	pedestrian underpass
sulphur(ous)	sulfur(ous)
sultana	golden (seedless) raisin
sweated (past tense and participle of sweat)	sweat

British	***American***
sweet shop	candy store
tap	faucet
tartan	plaid
terraced house	row house
till	checkout
titbit	tidbit
towards	toward
transport	transportation
trainers	sneakers
traveller/travelled	traveler/traveled
trousers	pants or slacks (trousers acceptable)
trunk call	long-distance call
turning (road)	turnoff
tyre	tire
underground (or tube train)	subway
upmarket	upscale
vest	undershirt
waistcoat	vest
walk	hike (only if more energetic than a walk)
water biscuit	cracker
way out	exit
woollen/woolly	woolen/wooly
work out (problem)	figure out
zip (n.)	zipper

Note than Teamster and Social Security have initial capitals in American English.

Differences in punctuation

Colons and capitals. When a colon precedes a full sentence (or question) rather than a phrase, Americans follow the colon with a capital letter. **The mystery was explained: The impala on the menu was an animal, not a car.** The British would treat this as a simple sentence with only an initial capital letter.

Commas in lists. Americans often put a comma before the **and: eggs, bacon, potatoes, and cheese**. The British usually write **eggs, bacon, potatoes and cheese.**

DASHES. In British publications, the usual style for a dash used as a parenthesis is an en-rule (–) with a character space either side. In American publications – and *The Economist* newspaper – the usual style for a dash is an em-rule (—) with no spaces.

FULL STOPS (PERIODS). The American convention is to use full stops (periods) to identify almost all abbreviations and contractions. The British convention is to keep them to a minimum.

QUOTATION MARKS. In American publications (and those of major Commonwealth countries), the convention is to use double quotation marks, reserving single quotation marks for quotes within quotes. In most British publications (excluding *The Economist*), the convention is the reverse: single quotation marks are used first, then double.

The relative position of quotation marks and other punctuation is far more contentious. The British convention is to place such punctuation according to sense. The American convention is simpler but less logical: all commas and full stops precede the final quotation mark (or, if there is a quote within a quote, the first final quotation mark). Other punctuation – colons, semi-colons, question and exclamation marks – is placed according to sense. The following examples illustrate these differences.

American style

The words on the magazine's cover, "The link between coffee and cholesterol," caught his eye.

"You're eating too much," she told him. "You'll soon look like your father."

"Have you seen this article, 'The link between coffee and cholesterol'?" he asked.

"It was as if," he explained, "I had swallowed a toad, and it kept croaking 'ribbut, ribbut,' from deep in my stomach."

She particularly enjoyed the article "Looking for the 'New Man.' "

British style

The words on the magazine's cover, 'The link between coffee and cholesterol', caught his eye.

'You're eating too much,' she told him. 'You'll soon look like your father.'

'Have you seen this article, "The link between coffee and cholesterol"?' he asked.

'It was as if', he explained, 'I had swallowed a toad, and it kept croaking "ribbut, ribbut", from deep in my belly.'

She particularly enjoyed the article 'Looking for the "New Man" '.

Different units of measurement

In British publications measurements are now largely expressed in SI units (the modern form of metric units), although imperial measures are still used in certain contexts. In American publications measurements may be expressed in SI or imperial units.

Although the British imperial and American standard measures are usually identical, there are some important exceptions. Some measures are peculiar to one or other national system, particularly units of mass relating to agriculture. See also MEASUREMENTS (Part I) and MEASURES (Part III).

Differences in accounting terminology

British	***American***
acquisition accounting	purchase accounting
articles of association	bylaws
balance sheet	statement of financial position
bills	notes

British	*American*
bonus or scrip issue	stock dividend or stock split
closing rate method	current rate method
creditors	payables
debtors	receivables
deferred tax	deferred income tax
depreciation	amortisation
exceptional items	unusual items
finance leases	capital leases
land and buildings	real estate
merger accounting	pooling of interests
nominal value	par value
non-pension post-employment benefits	OPEBs
ordinary shares	common stock
own shares purchased but not cancelled	Treasury stock
preference shares	preferred stock
profit and loss account	income statement
profit for the financial year	net income
provisions	allowances
share premium	additional paid-in capital
shareholders' funds	stockholders' equity
stocks	inventories
turnover	revenues
undistributable reserves	restricted surplus

PART III

FACT CHECKER AND GLOSSARY

A

ABBREVIATIONS.

Here is a list of some common business abbreviations.

See also ABBREVIATIONS, pages 6–7.

ABC	activity-based costing
ACH	automated clearing house
ACT	advance corporation tax (UK)
ADR	American depositary receipt
AG	Aktiengesellschaft (Austrian, German or Swiss public limited company)
AGM	annual general meeting
AIM	Alternative Investment Market (UK)
AMEX	American Stock Exchange
APR	annualised percentage rate (of interest)
ASSC	Accounting Standards Steering Committee (UK)
ATM	automated teller machine
B2B	business-to-business
B2C	business-to-consumer
CAPM	capital asset pricing model
CCA	current cost accounting
CD	certificate of deposit
CEDEL	Centre de livraison de valeurs mobilières
CEO	chief executive officer
CFO	chief financial officer
CGT	capital gains tax
cif	cost, insurance, freight
COB	Commission des Opérations de Bourse (Stock Exchange Commission, France)
Consob	Commissione Nazionale per le Società e la Borsa (Stock Exchange Commission, Italy)
COO	chief operating officer
COSA	cost of sales adjustment
CPA	certified public accountant (US); critical path analysis
CPP	current purchasing power (accounting)
CRC	current replacement cost
CVP	cost-volume-profit analysis
DCF	discounted cash flow
EBIT	earnings before interest and tax
EBITDA	earnings before interest, tax, depreciation and amortisation
EDP	electronic data processing

EFT electronic funds transfer
EFTPOS electronic funds transfer at point of sale
EMS European Monetary System
EMU economic and monetary union
EPS earnings per share
ESOP employee stock or share ownership plan
EV economic value
EVA economic value added
FASB Financial Accounting Standards Board (US)
FDI Foreign Direct Investment
FIFO first in, first out (used for valuing stock/inventory)
fob free on board
forex foreign exchange
FRN floating rate note
FSA Financial Services Authority
GAAP generally accepted accounting principles (US)
GAAS generally accepted audited standards
GDP gross domestic product
GmbH Gesellschaft mit beschränkter Haftung (Austrian, German or Swiss private limited company)
GNP gross national product
IPO initial public offering
IRR internal rate of return
IRS Internal Revenue Service (US)
JIT just-in-time
LAN local area network
LIBOR London Interbank Offered Rate
LIFFE London International Financial Futures Exchange
LIFO last in, first out (used for valuing stock/inventory value, popular in US)
M&A mergers and acquisitions
MATIF Marché à Terme des Instruments Financiers
MBI management buy-in
MBO management buy-out
MCT mainstream corporation tax
MLR minimum lending rate
NASDAQ National Association of Securities Dealers Automated Quotations System (US)
NBV net book value
NGO non-governmental organisation
NPV net present value; no par value
NRV net realisable value
Nymex New York Mercantile Exchange

NYSE	New York Stock Exchange
OTC	over the counter
P&L a/c	profit and loss account (known as the income statement in the US)
P/E	price/earnings (ratio)
PIN	personal identification number
PLC	public limited company (UK)
PPP	purchasing power parity
PSBR	public-sector borrowing rate
R&D	research and development
ROA	return on assets
ROCE	return on capital employed
ROE	return on equity
ROI	return on investment
RONA	return on net assets
ROOA	return on operating assets
ROTA	return on total assets
S&L	Savings and Loan Association (US)
SA	société anonyme (French, Belgian, Luxembourg or Swiss public limited company)
Sarl	société à responsabilité limitée (French, etc private limited company)
SDR	special drawing right (at the IMF)
SEAQ	Stock Exchange Automated Quotations (UK)
SEC	Securities and Exchange Commission (US)
SET	secure electronic transaction
SIB	Securities and Investments Board (UK)
SITC	standard international trade classification
SME	small and medium-sized enterprises
SpA	società per azioni (Italian public company)
SRO	self-regulating organisation
SSAP	Statement of Standard Accounting Practice (UK)
STRGL	statement of total recognised gains and losses
T-bill	Treasury bill
TQM	total quality management
TSR	total shareholder return
UEC	Union Européenne des Experts Comptables Economiques et Financiers
USM	Unlisted securities market (uk)
USP	unique selling proposition
VAT	value-added tax
WDV	written down value
WIP	work-in-progress

XBRL extensible business reporting language
ZBB zero base budgeting

For international bodies and their abbreviations, see ORGANISATIONS, pages 141ff.

ACCENTS. Here are some of the more familiar foreign-language accents.

acute	république
grave	grand'mère
circumflex	bête noire
umlaut	Länder, Österreich (Austria)
cedilla	français
tilde	señor, São Paulo

ACCOUNTANCY RATIOS.
These are the ratios most commonly used in accounting practice.

Working capital

Working capital ratio = current assets/current liabilities, where current assets = stock + debtors + cash at bank and in hand + quoted investments, etc, current liabilities = creditors + overdraft at bank + taxation + dividends, etc. The ratio varies according to type of trade and conditions; a ratio from 1 to 3 is usual with a ratio above 2 taken to be safe.
Liquidity ratio – liquid ("quick") assets/current liabilities, where liquid assets = debtors + cash at bank and in hand + quoted investments (that is assets which can be realised within a month or so, which may not apply to all investments); current liabilities are those which may need to be repaid within the same short period, which may not necessarily include a bank overdraft where it is likely to be renewed. The liquidity ratio is sometimes referred to as the "acid test"; a ratio under 1 suggests a possibly difficult situation, while too high a ratio may mean that assets are not being usefully employed.
Turnover of working capital = sales/average working capital. The ratio varies according to type of trade; generally a low ratio can mean poor use of resources, while too high a ratio can mean over-trading.
Turnover of stock = sales/average stock, or (where cost of sales is known) = cost of sales/average stock. The cost of sales turnover figure is to be preferred as both figures are then on the same valuation basis. This ratio can be expressed as number of times per year, or time taken for stock to be turned over once = (52/number of times) weeks. A low turnover of stock can be a sign of stocks which are difficult to move, and is usually a sign of adverse conditions.

Turnover of debtors = sales/average debtors. This indicates efficiency in collecting accounts. An average credit period of about one month is usual, but varies according to credit stringency conditions in the economy.
Turnover of creditors = purchases/average creditors. Average payment period is best maintained in line with turnover of debtors.

Sales

Export ratio = exports as a percentage of sales.
Sales per employee = sales/average number of employees.

Assets

Ratios of assets can vary according to the measure of assets used:
Total assets = current assets + fixed assets + other assets, where fixed assets = property + plant and machinery + motor vehicles, etc, and other assets = long-term investment + goodwill, etc.
Net assets ("net worth") = total assets − total liabilities
= share capital + reserves
Turnover of net assets = sales/average net assets. As for turnover of working capital, a low ratio can mean poor use of resources.
Assets per employee = assets/average number of employees. Indicates the amount of investment backing for employees.

Profits

Profit margin = (profit/sales) × 100 = profits as a percentage of sales; usually profits before tax.
Profitability = (profit/total assets) × 100 = profits as a percentage of total assets.
Return on capital = (profit/net assets) × 100 = profits as a percentage of net assets ("net worth" or "capital employed").
Profit per employee = profit/average number of employees.
Earnings per share (eps) = after-tax profit − minorities/average number of shares in issue.

B

Beaufort scale. The Beaufort Scale, once a picturesque fleet of well-scrubbed men-o'-war and fishing smacks, has been rendered bland by the World Meteorological Organization.

The Beaufort Scale

Conditions (abbreviated)				Equivalent speed at 10m height		
Force	Description	On land	At sea	knots	miles per hour	metres per second
0	Calm	Smoke rises vertically	Sea like a mirror	less than 1	less than 1	0.0–0.2
1	Light air	Smoke drifts	Ripples	1–3	1–3	0.3–1.5
2	Light breeze	Leaves rustle	Small wavelets	4–6	4–7	1.7–3.3
3	Gentle breeze	Wind extends light flag	Large wavelets, crests break	7–10	8–12	3.4–5.4
4	Moderate breeze	Raises paper and dust	Small waves, some white horses	11–16	13–18	5.5–7.9
5	Fresh breeze	Small trees in leaf sway	Moderate waves, many white horses	17–21	19–24	8.0–10.7
6	Strong breeze	Large branches in motion	Large waves form, some spray	22–27	25–31	10.8–13.8
7	Moderate gale or near gale	Whole trees in motion	Sea heaps up, white foam streaks	28–33	32–38	13.9–17.1
8	Fresh gale or gale	Breaks twigs off trees	Moderately high waves, well-marked foam streaks	34–40	39–46	17.2–20.7
9	Strong gale	Slight structural damage to tumble over	High waves, crests start	41–47	47–54	20.8–24.4
10	Whole gale or storm	Trees uprooted, considerable structural damage	Very high waves, white sea tumbles	48–55	55–63	24.5–28.4
11	Storm or violent storm	Very rarely experienced, widespread damage	Exceptionally high waves, edges of wave crests blown to froth	56–63	64–72	28.5–32.6
12–17	Hurricane	Devastation with driving spray	Sea completely white	64–118	73–136	32.7–over

C

CALENDARS. There are five important solar calendars.

Gregorian	Iranian[b]	Hindu[c]
January (31)[a]		
February (28 or 29)		
March (31)	Farvardin (31)	Caitra (30)
April (30)	Ordibehesht (31)	Vaisakha (31)
May (31)	Khordad (31)	Jyaistha (31)
June (30)	Tir (31)	Asadha (31)
July (31)	Mordad (31)	Sravana (31)
August (31)	Shahrivar (31)	Bhadrapada (31)
September (30)	Mehr (30)	Asvina (30)
October (31)	Aban (30)	Karttika (30)
November (30)	Azar (30)	Margasirsa (30)
December (31)	Dey (30)	Pausa (30)
January	Bahman (30)	Magha (30)
February	Esfand (28 or 29)	Phalguna (30)

Gregorian	Ethiopian[d]	Jewish[e]
September	Meskerem (30)	Tishri (30)
October	Tikemet (30)	Heshvan (29 or 30)
November	Hidar (30)	Kislev (29 or 30)
December	Tahesas (30)	Tebet (29)
January	Tir (30)	Shebat (30)
February	Yekatit (30)	Adar (29)
March	Megabit (30)	Nisan (30)
April	Miyaza (30)	Iyar (29)
May	Ginbot (30)	Sivan (30)
June	Sene (30)	Tammuz (29)
July	Hamle (30)	Ab (30)
August	Nehase (30+5 or 6)	Elul (29)
	Paguma	

a Figures in brackets denote the number of days in that month.

b Months begin about the 21st of the corresponding Gregorian month.

c Months begin about the 22nd of the corresponding Gregorian month.

d Months begin on the 11th of the corresponding Gregorian month.

e The date of the new year varies, but normally falls in the second half of September in the Gregorian calendar; the position is maintained by sometimes adding an extra period of 29 days, Adar Sheni, following the month of Adar. The Jewish calendar is a combined solar/lunar calendar, like the Chinese.

The Muslim calendar. Muslims use a lunar calendar which begins 10 or 11 days earlier each year in terms of the Gregorian. The months, whose names follow, do not have a fixed number of days. In each 30 years, 19 years have 354 days (are "common") and 11 have 355 days (are "intercalary").

Muharram	Rajab
Safar	Sha'ban
Rabi' I	Ramadan
Rabi' II	Shawwal
Jumada I	Dhu al-Qidah
Jumada II	Dhu al-Hijjah

The Muslim years in the columns below begin on the dates of the Gregorian calendar as shown.

1413	July 2nd 1992	1420	April 17th 1999
1414	June 21st 1993	1421	April 6th 2000
1415	June 9th 1994	1422	March 26th 2001
1416	May 31st 1995	1423	March 15th 2002
1417	May 19th 1996	1424	March 5th 2003
1418	May 9th 1997	1425	February 22nd 2004
1419	April 28th 1998	1426	February 10th 2005

Cars.

Here is a list of international vehicle registration (IVR) letters.

A	Austria	**BH**	Belize
ADN	Yemen	**BIH**	Bosnia & Hercegovina
AFG	Afghanistan	**BOL**	Bolivia
AG	Antigua And Barbuda	**BR**	Brazil
AL	Albania	**BRN**	Bahrain
AND	Andorra	**BRU**	Brunei
AO	Angola	**BS**	Bahamas
ARM	Armenia	**BTN**	Bhutan
AUS	Australia	**BUR**	Myanmar
AZ	Azerbaijan	**C**	Cuba
B	Belgium	**CAM**	Cameroon
BD	Bangladesh	**CDN**	Canada
BDA	Bermuda	**CH**	Switzerland
BDS	Barbados	**CI**	Côte d'Ivoire
BF	Burkina Faso	**CL**	Sri Lanka
BG	Bulgaria	**CO**	Colombia

CR	Costa Rica
CY	Cyprus
CZ	Czech Republic
D	Germany
DK	Denmark
DOM	Dominican Republic
DY	Benin
DZ	Algeria
E	Spain
EAK	Kenya
EAT	Tanzania
EAU	Uganda
EC	Ecuador
ES	El Salvador
EST	Estonia
ET	Egypt
ETH	Ethiopia
F	France
FIN	Finland
FJI	Fiji
FL	Liechtenstein
FO	Faroe Islands
GB	Great Britain
GBA	Alderney
GBG	Guernsey
GBJ	Jersey
GBM	Isle of Man
GBZ	Gibraltar
GCE	Guatemala
GE	Georgia
GH	Ghana
GR	Greece
GUY	Guyana
H	Hungary
HK	Hong Kong
HKJ	Jordan
HR	Croatia
I	Italy
IL	Israel
IND	India
IR	Iran
IRL	Ireland
IRQ	Iraq
IS	Iceland
J	Japan
JA	Jamaica
K	Cambodia (Kampuchea)
KS	Kirgizstan
KWT	Kuwait
KZ	Kazakhstan
L	Luxembourg
LAO	Laos
LAR	Libya
LB	Liberia
LS	Lesotho
LT	Lithuania
LV	Latvia
M	Malta
MA	Morocco
MAL	Malaysia
MC	Monaco
MD	Moldova
MEX	Mexico
MS	Mauritius
MW	Malawi
MKFYR	Macedonia (FYROM)
MZ	Mozambique
N	Norway
NA	Netherlands Antilles
NAM	Namibia
NIC	Nicaragua
NL	Netherlands
NZ	New Zealand
P	Portugal
PA	Panama
PE	Peru
PK	Pakistan
PL	Poland
PNG	Papua New Guinea
PY	Paraguay
QA	Qatar
RA	Argentina
RB	Botswana
RC	China
RCA	Central African Rep.

RCB	Congo	**T**	Thailand
RCH	Chile	**TG**	Togo
RH	Haiti	**TJ**	Tajikistan
RI	Indonesia	**TM**	Turkmenistan
RIM	Mauritania	**TN**	Tunisia
RL	Lebanon	**TR**	Turkey
RM	Madagascar	**TT**	Trinidad &Tobago
RMM	Mali	**UA**	Ukraine
RN	Niger	**UAE**	United Arab Emirates
RO	Romania	**USA**	United States
ROK	South Korea	**UZ**	Uzbekistan
ROU	Uruguay	**V**	Vatican
RP	Philippines	**VN**	Vietnam
RSM	San Marino	**WAG**	The Gambia
RUS	Russia	**WAL**	Sierra Leone
RU	Burundi	**WAN**	Nigeria
RWA	Rwanda	**WD**	Dominica
S	Sweden	**WG**	Grenada
SA	Saudi Arabia	**WL**	St Lucia
SD	Swaziland	**WS**	West Samoa
SGP	Singapore	**WV**	St Vincent and Grenadines
SK	Slovakia	**YU**	Yugoslavia
SLO	Slovenia	**YV**	Venezuela
SME	Suriname	**Z**	Zambia
SN	Senegal	**ZA**	South Africa
SU	Belarus	**ZRE**	Congo, Dem. Rep. of
SUD	Sudan	**ZW**	Zimbabwe
SY	Seychelles		
SYR	Syria		

Cities. Below is a list of the 50 largest urban agglomerations in the world, of which Tokyo is the biggest and Toronto the smallest. Those marked [a] are capital cities.

Ahmadabad	*India*	Chennai	*India*
Bangalore	*India*	Chicago	*US*
Bangkok	*Thailand*	Chongqing	*China*
Beijing[a]	*China*	Dallas	*US*
Belo Horizonte	*Brazil*	Delhi[a]	*India*
Bogotá[a]	*Colombia*	Detroit	*US*
Boston	*US*	Dhaka	*Bangladesh*
Buenos Aires[a]	*Argentina*	Essen	*Germany*
Cairo[a]	*Egypt*	Hong Kong	*China*

Hyderabad	*India*	Mumbai	*India*
Istanbul	*Turkey*	New York	*US*
Jakarta[a]	*Indonesia*	Osaka	*Japan*
Johannesburg	*South Africa*	Paris[a]	*France*
Karachi	*Pakistan*	Philadelphia	*US*
Khartoum	*Egypt*	Rio de Janeiro	*Brazil*
Kinshasa[a]	*Congo, Dem. Rep.*	San Francisco	*US*
Kolkata	*India*	São Paulo[a]	*Brazil*
Lagos[a]	*Nigeria*	Seoul[a]	*South Korea*
Lahore	*Pakistan*	Shanghai	*China*
Lima[a]	*Peru*	St Petersburg	*Russia*
London[a]	*UK*	Taipei[a]	*Taiwan*
Los Angeles	*US*	Tehran[a]	*Iran*
Manila[a]	*Philippines*	Tianjin	*China*
Mexico City[a]	*Mexico*	Tokyo[a]	*Japan*
Moscow[a]	*Russia*	Washington, DC[a]	*US*

Commodities and manufactured goods.
Most countries use the Standard International Trade Classification (SITC) to describe the goods they import and trade. The classifications are periodically revised: SITC (3) was introduced in January 1988. A list of the main items follows.

There are 9 sections, giving single digits 1–9; divisions within these sections have 2-digit numbers, and groups within each division have 3-digit numbers. In the list below all sections and divisions are shown together with selected groups. There are also 4-digit sub-groups in the SITC list, with, for example, 072.3 for "cocoa paste" as a subgroup of 072 ("cocoa"), and further breakdowns for some items into a 5-digit level, with, for example, 072.32 for "cocoa paste, wholly or partly defatted". Throughout, nes stands for "not elsewhere specified".

0	Food and live animals
00	Live animals
01	Meat and meat preparations
001	Live animals other than animals of division 03
02	Dairy products and birds' eggs
022	Milk, cream, milk products, excluding butter or cheese
023	Butter and other fats and oils derived from milk
024	Cheese and curd
03	Fish
037	Fish, crustaceans, etc, prepared or preserved
04	Cereals
041	Wheat, including spelt, and meslin, unmilled

042	Rice
043	Barley, unmilled
044	Maize not including sweetcorn, unmilled
05	Vegetables and fruit
057	Fruit and nuts, excluding oil nuts, fresh or dried
06	Sugars and honey
062	Sugar confectionery
07	Coffee, tea, cocoa and spices
071	Coffee and coffee substitutes
072	Cocoa
074	Tea and maté
08	Animal feed
09	Miscellaneous edible products
1	Beverages and tobacco
11	Beverages
112	Alcoholic beverages
12	Tobacco
2	Crude materials, inedible, except fuels
21	Hides, skins and furskins
212	Furskins, raw
22	Oil seeds and oleaginous fruit
23	Crude rubber
24	Cork and wood
245	Fuel wood and wood charcoal, excluding wood waste
25	Pulp and waste paper
26	Textile fibres and waste
263	Cotton textile fibres
266	Synthetic fibres suitable for spinning
268	Wool and other animal hair (including wool tops)
27	Crude fertilisers
273	Stone, sand and gravel
28	Metalliferous ores and metal scrap
281	Iron ore and concentrates
29	Crude animal and vegetable materials
3	Mineral fuels, lubricants and related materials
32	Coal, coke and briquettes
33	Petroleum and petroleum products
333	Crude oil from petroleum or bituminous materials
34	Gas, natural and manufactured
35	Electric current

4 Animal and vegetable oils, fats and waxes
41 Animal oils and fats
42 Fixed vegetable fats and oils
43 Animal fats, vegetable oils and waxes

5 Chemical and related products, nes
51 Organic chemicals
52 Inorganic chemicals
53 Dyeing, tanning and colouring materials
54 Medicinal and pharmaceutical products
55 Oils, perfumes and soaps
554 Soap, cleansing and polishing preparations
56 Fertilisers
57 Plastics in primary forms
58 Plastics in non-primary forms
59 Chemical materials and products

6 Manufactured goods, classified chiefly by material
61 Leather and leather manufactures
62 Rubber manufactures
63 Cork and wood manufactures
64 Paper
65 Textile yarn and fabric
66 Non-metallic mineral manufactures
67 Iron and steel
68 Non-ferrous metals
681 Silver, platinum and other metals of the platinum group
682 Copper
683 Nickel
684 Aluminium
685 Lead
686 Zinc
687 Tin
69 Manufactures of metal

7 Machinery and transport equipment
71 Power generating machinery
713 Internal combustion piston engines, and parts thereof
72 Specialised machinery
721 Agricultural machinery and parts, excluding tractors
724 Textile and leather machinery, and parts thereof
73 Metalworking machinery
74 Industrial machinery

75	Office and automatic data processing (ADP) machines
76	Telecommunications equipment
761	Television receivers
763	Sound recorders, TV recorders, prepared unrecorded media
77	Electrical machinery
78	Road vehicles
781	Motor cars and other motor vehicles
782	Motor vehicles for transport of goods and special purpose motor vehicles
79	Transport equipment
791	Railway vehicles and associated equipment
792	Aircraft and associated equipment, and parts thereof; spacecraft
793	Ships, boats and floating structures
8	Miscellaneous manufactured articles
81	Prefabricated buildings and fixtures
82	Furniture and bedding
83	Travel goods and handbags
831	Trunks, suitcases, vanity cases, briefcases, etc
84	Apparel
841	Men's or boys' coats, jackets, etc, of textile fabrics, not knitted
85	Footwear
87	Professional and scientific instruments
871	Optical instruments and apparatus
88	Photo equipment, watches and clocks
881	Photographic apparatus and equipment
885	Watches and clocks
89	Miscellaneous manufactured goods
895	Office and stationery supplies
9	Commodities and transactions, nes
91	Miscellaneous postal packages
911	Postal packages not classified according to kind
931	Special transactions and commodities not classified according to kind
961	Coin (other than gold coin) not being legal tender
981	Military arms and ammunitions

CURRENCIES.[a]

Country	*Currency*	*Symbol*
Afghanistan	afghani	Af
Albania	lek	Lk
Algeria	New (Algerian) dinar	AD
Angola	kwanza	NKz
Argentina	peso	Ps
Armenia	dram	Dram
Aruba	Aruban florin	Afl
Australia	Australian dollar	A$
Austria	euro	€
Azerbaijan	manat	Manat
Bahamas	Bahamian dollar	B$
Bahrain	Bahraini dinar	BD
Bangladesh	taka	Tk
Barbados	Barbados dollar	Bd$
Belarus	Belarusian rouble	BRb
Belgium	euro	€
Belize	Belize dollar	Bz$
Benin	CFA franc	CFAfr[b]
Bermuda	Bermuda dollar	Bda$
Bolivia	boliviano	Bs
Bosnia & Hercegovina	Bosnia & Hercegovina dinar	BiHD
Botswana	pula	P
Brazil	*real* (pl. *reais*)	R
Brunei	Brunei dollar/ringgit	Br$
Bulgaria	lev	Lv
Burkina Faso	CFA franc	CFAfr
Burundi	Burundi franc	Bufr
Cambodia	riel	CR
Cameroon	CFA franc	CFAfr
Canada	Canadian dollar	C$
Cape Verde	Cape Verde escudo	CVEsc
Central African Republic	CFA franc	CFAfr
Chad	CFA franc	CFAfr
Chile	Chilean peso	Ps
China	renminbi	Rmb
Colombia	Colombian peso	Ps
Comoros	Comorian franc	Cfr
Congo (Brazzaville)	CFA franc	CFAfr
Congo (Dem. Rep. of)	nouveau zaïre	NZ

Country	*Currency*	*Symbol*
Costa Rica	Costa Rican colón	C
Côte d'Ivoire	CFA franc	CFAfr
Croatia	kuna	HRK
Cuba	Cuban peso	Ps
Cyprus	Cyprus pound/Turkish lira	C£/TL
Czech Republic	koruna	Kc
Denmark	Danish krone	DKr
Djibouti	Djibouti franc	Dfr
Dominican Republic	Dominican Republic peso	Ps
Dubai	UAE dirham	Dh
Ecuador	sucre	Su
Egypt	Egyptian pound	£E
El Salvador	El Salvador colón	c
Equatorial Guinea	CFA franc	CFAfr
Estonia	kroon	EEK
Ethiopia	birr	Birr
European Union	euro	€
Fiji	Fiji dollar	F$
Finland	euro	€
France	euro	€
Gabon	CFA franc	CFAfr
The Gambia	dalasi	D
Georgia	lari	Lari
Germany	euro	€
Ghana	cedi	C
Greece	euro	€
Grenada	East Caribbean dollar	EC$
Guatemala	quetzal	Q
Guinea	Guinean franc	Gnf
Guinea-Bissau	CFA franc	CFAfr
Guyana	Guyanese dollar	G$
Haiti	gourde	G
Honduras	lempira	La
Hong Kong	Hong Kong dollar	HK$
Hungary	forint	Ft
Iceland	Iceland new króna	Ikr
India	Indian rupee	Rs
Indonesia	rupiah	Rp
Iran	rial	IR
Iraq	Iraqi dinar	ID
Ireland	euro	€

Country	*Currency*	*Symbol*
Israel	New Israeli shekel	NIS
Italy	euro	€
Jamaica	Jamaican dollar	J$
Japan	yen	¥
Jordan	Jordanian dinar	JD
Kazakhstan	tenge	Tenge
Kenya	Kenya shilling	KSh
Kirgizstan	som	Som
North Korea	won	Won
South Korea	won	W
Kuwait	Kuwaiti dinar	KD
Laos	kip	K
Latvia	lat	LVL
Lebanon	Lebanese pound	L£
Lesotho	loti (pl. maloti)	M
Liberia	Liberian dollar	L$
Libya	Libyan dinar	LD
Lithuania	lit	LTL
Luxembourg	euro	€
Macau	pataca	MPtc
Macedonia	Macedonian denar	Den
Malagasy	Malagasy franc	Mgfr
Malawi	kwacha	MK
Malaysia	Malaysian dollar/ringgit	M$
Mali	CFA franc	CFAfr
Malta	Maltese lira	Lm
Mauritania	ouguiya	UM
Mauritius	Mauritius rupee	MRs
Mexico	Mexican peso	Ps
Moldova	Moldavian leu (pl. lei)	Lei
Mongolia	togrog	Tg
Morocco	dirham	Dh
Mozambique	metical	MT
Myanmar	kyat	Kt
Namibia	Namibia dollar	N$
Nepal	Nepalese rupee	NRs
Netherlands	euro	€
Netherlands Antilles	Netherlands Antilles guilder	NAG
New Caledonia	French Pacific franc	CFPfr
New Zealand	New Zealand dollar	NZ$
Nicaragua	córdoba	C

Country	*Currency*	*Symbol*
Niger	CFA franc	CFAfr
Nigeria	naira	N
Norway	Norwegian krone	NKr
Occupied Territories	Jordanian dinar, New Israeli shekel	JD, NIS
Oman	Omani rial	OR
Pakistan	Pakistan rupee	PRs
Panama	balboa	B
Papua New Guinea	kina	Kina
Paraguay	guarani	G
Peru	nuevo sol	Ns
Philippines	Philippine peso	P
Poland	zloty (pl. zlotys)	Zl
Portugal	euro	€
Puerto Rico	US dollar	US$
Qatar	Qatari riyal	QR
Romania	leu (pl. lei)	Lei
Russia	rouble	Rb
Rwanda	Rwandan franc	Rwfr
São Tomé & Príncipe	dobra	Db
Saudi Arabia	Saudi riyal	SR
Senegal	CFA franc	CFAfr
Serbia-Montenegro	Yugoslav dinar	YuD
Seychelles	Seychelles rupee	SRs
Sierra Leone	leone	Le
Singapore	Singapore dollar	S$
Slovakia	Slovak koruna	Sk
Slovenia	tolar	SIT
Solomon Islands	Solomon Islands dollar	SI$
Somalia	Somali shilling	SoSh
South Africa	rand	R
Spain	euro	€
Sri Lanka	Sri Lanka rupee	SLRs
Sudan	Sudanese pound/dinar	S£/SD
Suriname	Suriname guilder	SG
Swaziland	lilangeni (pl. emalangeni)	E
Sweden	Swedish krona	SKr
Switzerland	Swiss franc	Swfr
Syria	Syrian pound	S£
Taiwan	New Taiwan dollar	NT$
Tajikistan	Tajik rouble	TR

Country	*Currency*	*Symbol*
Tanzania	Tanzanian shilling	TSh
Thailand	baht	Bt
Togo	CFA franc	CFAfr
Tonga	Tonga dollar	T$
Trinidad & Tobago	TT dollar	TT$
Tunisia	Tunisian dinar	TD
Turkey	Turkish lira	TL
Turkmenistan	manat	Manat
Uganda	New Ugandan shilling	NUSh
Ukraine	hryvnya	HRN
United Arab Emirates	UAE dirham	Dh
United Kingdom	pound/sterling	£
United States	dollar	$
Uruguay	Uruguayan new peso	Ps
Uzbekistan	som	Som
Vanuatu	vatu	Vt
Venezuela	bolívar	Bs
Vietnam	dong	D
Western Samoa	tala	Tala
Windward & Leeward Islands[c]	East Caribbean dollar	EC$
Yemen	Yemeni rial	YR
Yugoslavia (Serbia-Montenegro)	Yugoslav dinar	YuD
Zambia	kwacha	ZK
Zimbabwe	Zimbabwe dollar	Z$

a See CURRENCIES, pages 22–23, for *The Economist* newspaper usage.

b CFA = Communauté financière africaine in West African area and Coopération financière en Afrique centrale in Central African area. Used in monetary areas of West and Central Africa. 1 franc CFA = 1 French centime.

c Antigua and Barbuda, Dominica, Grenada, Monserrat, St Kitts-Nevis, St Lucia, St Vincent & Grenadines, the British Virgin islands.

E

EARTHQUAKES. The Richter scale defines the magnitude of an earthquake in terms of the energy released.

Richter scale		*Explosion equivalent*	
	Joules	TNT *terms*	*Nuclear terms*
0[a]	7.9×10^{2}	175mg	
1	6.0×10^{4}	13g	
2	4.0×10^{6}	0.89kg	
3	2.4×10^{8}	53kg	
4	1.3×10^{10}	3 tons	
5[b]	6.3×10^{11}	140 tons	
6[c]	2.7×10^{13}	6 kilotons	⅓ atomic bomb
7	1.1×10^{15}	240 kilotons	12 atomic bombs
8	3.7×10^{16}	8.25 megatons	⅓ hydrogen bomb
9	1.1×10^{18}	250 megatons	13 hydrogen bombs
10	3.2×10^{19}	7,000 megatons	350 hydrogen bombs

a About equal to the shock caused by an average man jumping from a table.

b Potentially damaging to structures.

c Potentially capable of general destruction; widespread damage is usually caused above magnitude 6.5.

Note: One atomic bomb is equivalent to 6.3 on the Richter scale, and one hydrogen bomb to 8.2.

Here are some examples.

	Richter scale		*Richter scale*
Ceram Sea, 1998	8.3	Ecuador, 1906	8.8
Kuril Islands, 1994	8.3	Colombia, 1906	8.9
San Francisco, 1906	8.3	Sanrika, Japan, 1933	8.9
Chile, 1906	8.6	Kamchatka, 1952	9.0
Gansu, China, 1920	8.6	Alaska, 1964	9.2
Kangra, India, 1905	8.6	Aleutian Islands, 1957	9.2
Aleutian Islands, 1965	8.7	Chile, 1960	9.5
India/Assam/Tibet, 1950	8.7	Krakatoa, 1883	9.9
Balleny Islands, 1998	8.8	(estimate)	

ELEMENTS.
These are the natural and artificially created chemical elements.

Name	*Symbol*	*Name*	*Symbol*
Actinium	Ac	Hassium	Hs
Aluminium	Al	Helium	He
Americium	Am	Holmium	Ho
Antimony (Stibium)	Sb	Hydrogen	H
Argon	Ar	Indium	In
Arsenic	As	Iodine	I
Astatine	At	Iridium	Ir
Barium	Ba	Iron (Ferrum)	Fe
Berkelium	Bk	Krypton	Kr
Beryllium	Be	Lanthanum	La
Bismuth	Bi	Lawrencium	Lw
Bohrium	Bh	Lead (Plumbum)	Pb
Boron	B	Lithium	Li
Bromine	Br	Lutetium	Lu
Cadmium	Cd	Magnesium	Mg
Caesium	Cs	Manganese	Mn
Calcium	Ca	Meitnerium	Mt
Californium	Cf	Mendelevium	Md
Carbon	C	Mercury (Hydrargyrum)	Hg
Cerium	Ce	Molybdenum	Mo
Chlorine	Cl	Neodymium	Nd
Chromium	Cr	Neon	Ne
Cobalt	Co	Neptunium	Np
Copper (Cuprum)	Cu	Nickel	Ni
Curium	Cm	Niobium (Columbium)	Nb
Dubnium	Db	Nitrogen	N
Dysprosium	Dy	Nobelium	No
Einsteinium	Es	Osmium	Os
Erbium	Er	Oxygen	O
Europium	Eu	Palladium	Pd
Fermium	Fm	Phosphorus	P
Fluorine	F	Platinum	Pt
Francium	Fr	Plutonium	Pu
Gadolinium	Gd	Polonium	Po
Gallium	Ga	Potassium (Kalium)	K
Germanium	Ge	Praseodymium	Pr
Gold (Aurum)	Au	Promethium	Pm
Hafnium	Ha	Protactinium	Pa

Name	*Symbol*	*Name*	*Symbol*
Radium	Ra	Terbium	Tb
Radon	Rn	Thallium	Tl
Rhenium	Re	Thorium	Th
Rhodium	Rh	Thulium	Tm
Rubidium	Rb	Tin (Stannum)	Sn
Ruthenium	Ru	Titanium	Ti
Rutherfordium	Rf	Tungsten (Wolfram)	W
Samarium	Sm	Ununbium	Uub
Scandium	Sc	Ununhexium	Uuh
Seaborgium	Sg	Ununnilium	Uun
Selenium	Se	Ununquadium	Uuq
Silicon	Si	Unununium	Uuu
Silver (Argentum)	Ag	Uranium	U
Sodium (Natrium)	Na	Vanadium	V
Strontium	Sr	Xenon	Xe
Sulphur	S	Ytterbium	Yb
Tantalum	Ta	Yttrium	Y
Technetium	Tc	Zinc	Zn
Tellurium	Te	Zirconium	Zr

F

FRACTIONS. Do not mingle fractions with decimals. If you need to convert one to the other, use this table. See also FIGURES, pages 29–30.

Fraction	*Decimal equivalent*
1/2	0.5
1/3	0.333
1/4	0.25
1/5	0.2
1/6	0.167
1/7	0.143
1/8	0.125
1/9	0.111
1/10	0.1
1/11	0.091
1/12	0.083
1/13	0.077
1/14	0.071
1/15	0.067
1/16	0.063
1/17	0.059
1/18	0.056
1/19	0.053
1/20	0.05

G

GEOLOGICAL ERAS. Astronomers and geologists give this broad outline of the ages of the universe and the earth.

Era, period and epoch		*Years ago m*	*Characteristics*
Origin of the universe (estimates vary markedly)		20,000–10,000	
Origin of the sun		5,000	
Origin of the earth		4,600	
Pre-Cambrian			
Archean		4,000	First signs of fossilised microbes
Proterozoic		2,500	
Palaeozoic			
Cambrian		570	First appearance of abundant fossils
Ordovician (obsolete)		500	Vertebrates emerge
Silurian		440	Fishes emerge
Devonian		400	Primitive plants emerge
Carboniferous		350	Amphibians emerge
Permian		270	Reptiles emerge
Mesozoic			
Triassic		250	Seed plants emerge
Jurassic		210	Age of dinosaurs
Cretaceous		145	Flowering plants emerge; dinosaurs extinct at end of this period
Cenozoic			
Palaeocene		65	
Tertiary:	Eocene	55	Mammals emerge
	Oligocene	40	
	Miocene	25	
	Pliocene	5	
Quaternary:	Pleistocene	2	Ice ages; stone age man emerges
	Holocene or Recent	c.10,000[a]	Modern man emerges

a 10,000 years, not 10,000m years.

I

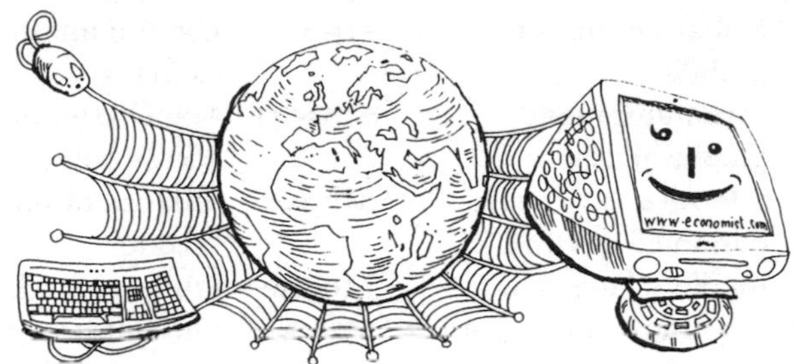

INTERNET. Here is a list of abbreviations commonly used in connection with the internet.

ADSL asynchronous digital subscriber line
AIML artificial intelligence mark-up language
AOL America Online
ASP application service provider
ATM asynchronous transfer mode or adobe type manager
BBS bulletin board system
BCC blind carbon copy
BPS bits per second
BRI basic rate interface
CAD computer aided design
CC carbon copy
CCS cascading style sheet
CDA communications decency act
CDF channel definition format
CGI common gateway interface
COM component object model
CORBA common object request broker architecture
DCOM distributed component object model
DES data encryption standard
DHCP dynamic host configuration protocol
DHTML dynamic hypertext mark-up language
DOM document object model
DNS domain name system
DSL digital subscriber line (or loop)
EDI electronic data interchange
EFF electronic frontier foundation
FAQ frequently asked questions
FDM frequency-division multiplexing
FSF free software foundation
FTP file transfer protocol
GIF graphics interchange format

GPRS general packet radio service
GSM global system for mobile communications
GUI graphical user interface
HDML handheld devices mark-up language
HTCPCP hyper text coffee pot control protocol
HTML hypertext mark-up language
HTTP hypertext transfer protocol
IAB internet architecture board
IANA internet assigned names authority
ICANN internet corporation for assigned names and numbers
ICQ I seek you
IETF internet engineering task force
IM instant messaging
IMAP internet message access protocol
IOTP internet open trading protocol
IP internet protocol
IRC internet relay chat
IRL in real life
ISDN integrated services digital network
ISP internet service provider
JANET joint academic network
JPEG joint picture experts group (or **JPG**)
Kbps kilobits per second
LAN local area network
LDAP lightweight directory access protocol
LINX London internet exchange
MANAP Manchester network access point
Mbps millions of bits per second
Mbone multicast backbone
MIME multipurpose internet mail extensions
MIP mobile internet protocol
MOO MUD Object Oriented
MSN Microsoft network
MPEG motion picture experts group
MUD multi-user dungeon
NAP network access point
NC network computer
NCSA National Centre for Supercomputing Applications
NNTP network news transport protocol
OPS open profiling standard
ORB object request broker
OS operating system
OSI open source initiative
PANS public access network services
PCS personal communications service
PDA personal digital assistant
PDF portable document format
PGP pretty good privacy
PKI public key infrastructure
PICS platform for internet content selection

POP	point of presence
POP3	post office protocol (latest version)
POTS	plain old telephone service
PPP	point-to-point protocol
PRI	primary rate interface
PVC	permanent virtual circuit
QOS	quality of service
RFC	request for comments
RSAC	Recreational Software Advisory Council
SDMI	secure digital music initiative
SMTP	simple mail transport protocol
SOAP	simple access object protocol
SQL	structured query language
SSL	secure sockets layer
TCP	transmission control protocol
TCP/IP	transmission control protocol/internet protocol
TDM	time-division multiplexing
TLA	three-letter acronym
TLD	top-level domain
TTP	trusted third party
UDDI	universal description, discovery and integration
UDRP	uniform dispute resolution policy
URI	uniform resource identifier
URL	uniform resource locator
UUCP	unix-to-unix copy protocol
UWB	ultra-wideband
VBNS	very high speed backbone network service
VISP	virtual internet service provider
VM	virtual machine
VOIP	voice over IP
VPN	virtual private network
VRML	virtual reality modelling language
W3C	world wide web consortium
WAP	wireless application protocol
WASP	wireless application service provider
WDM	wavelength-division multiplexing
WELL	whole earth 'lectronic link
WEP	wired equivalent privacy
Wi-Fi	wireless fidelity
WMA	windows media audio
WML	wireless mark-up language
WSDL	web services description language
WWW	world wide web
XHTML	extensible hypertext mark-up language
XML	extensible mark-up language
XSL	extensible stylesheet language
XTLA	extended three-letter acronym

L

LATIN.

Here are some common Latin words and phrases, together with their translations.

ab initio from the beginning
ad hoc for this object or purpose (implied and "this one only"); therefore, without a system, spontaneously
ad hominem to an individual's interests or passions; used of an argument that takes advantage of the character of the person on the other side
ad infinitum to infinity, that is, endlessly
ad lib. ***ad libitum***, meaning at pleasure. Used adverbially or even as a verb when it means to invent or extemporise
ad valorem according to value (as opposed to volume)
a fortiori with stronger reason
annus mirabilis wonderful year, used to describe a special year, one in which more than one memorable thing has happened; for instance 1666, the year of the Great Fire of London and the English defeats of the Dutch
a priori from cause to effect, that is, deductively or from prior principle
cave "Watch out!" (imperative); once used at boys' private schools in Britain
caveat emptor let the buyer beware
ceteris paribus other things being equal
cf short for ***confer***, meaning compare
circa around or about: used for dates and large quantities; can be abbreviated to **c** or **c.**
de facto in point of fact
de jure from the law; by right
de profundis from the depths
deus ex machina God from a machine; first used of a Greek theatrical convention, where a god would swing on to the stage, high up in a machine, solving humanly insoluble problems and thus resolving the action of a play. Now used to describe a wholly outside person who puts matters right
eg ***exempli gratia***, for example
et al. ***et alii***, and others, used as an abbreviation in bibliographies when citing multiple editorship or authorship to save the writer the bother of writing out all the names. Thus, A. Bloggs *et al.*, *The Occurrence of Endangered Species in the Genus Orthodoptera*

ex cathedra from the chair of office, authoritatively
ex officio by virtue of one's office, not unofficially
ex parte from or for one side only
ibid. ***ibidem***, in the same place; used in footnotes in academic works to mean that the quote comes from the same source
idem the same, that is mentioned before; like ***ibidem***
ie ***id est***, that is, explains the material immediately in front of it
in absentia in the absence of, used as "absent"
in camera in a (private) room, that is, not in public
in re in the matter of
in situ in (its) original place
inter alia/inter alios among other things or people
ipso facto by that very fact, in the fact itself
loc. cit. ***loco citato***, in the place cited; used in footnotes to mean that the source of the reference or quote has already been given
mea culpa my fault
mirabile dictu literally, wonderful to relate
mutatis mutandis after making the necessary changes
nem. con. ***nemine contradicente***, no one against; unanimously
op. cit. ***opere citato***, in the work quoted; similar to ***loc. cit.*** (q.v.)
pace despite
pari passu on the same terms, at an equal pace or rate of progress
passim adverb, here and there or scattered. Used in indexes to indicate that the item is scattered throughout the work and there are too many instances to enumerate them all
per se by itself, for its own sake
persona non grata person not in favour
per stirpes among families. A lawyer's term used when distributing an inheritance
petitio elenchis the sin of assuming a conclusion
post eventum after the event
post hoc, ergo propter hoc after this, therefore because of this. Used fallaciously in argument to show that because something comes after something it can be inferred that the first thing caused the second thing
post mortem after death, used as an adjective and also as a noun, a clinical examination of a dead body
prima facie from a first impression, apparently at first sight, – no connection with love
primus inter pares first among equals
pro tem. ***pro tempore***, for the moment
PS ***post scriptum***, written afterwards

quid pro quo something for something (or one thing for another), something in return, an equivalent; usually given
q.v. ***quod vide***, which see; means that the reader should look for the word just mentioned (eg in glossary)
re with regard to, in the matter of
sic thus; used in brackets in quotes to show writer has made a mistake. "Mrs Thacher (sic) resigned today."
sine die without (setting) a date
sine qua non without which, not. Anything indispensable, and without which another cannot exist
status quo ante the same state as before; usually shortened to ***status quo***. A common usage is "maintaining the status quo"
stet let it stand or do not delete; cancels an alteration in proof-reading; dots are placed under what is to remain
sub judice under judgment or consideration; not yet decided
sub rosa under the rose, privately or furtively; not the same as under the gooseberry bush
ultra vires beyond (one's) legal power
vade mecum a little book or something carried about on the person; literally "Go with me"
Vae victis Woe to the conquered! A Roman phrase
versus shortened to **v** or **v.**, against; used in legal cases and games

Laws.

Scientific, economic, facetious and fatalistic laws in common use are listed here.

Boyle's Law. The pressure of a gas varies inversely with its volume at constant temperature.

Gresham's Law. When money of a high intrinsic value is in circulation with money of lesser value, it is the inferior currency which tends to remain in circulation, while the other is either hoarded or exported. In other words: "Bad money drives out good".

Grimm's Law. Concerns mutations of the consonants in the various Germanic languages. Proto-Indo-European voiced aspirated stops, voiced unaspirated stops and voiceless stops become respectively voiced unaspirated stops, voiceless stops and voiceless fricatives.

Heisenberg's Uncertainty Principle. Energy and time or position and momentum cannot both be accurately measured simultaneously. The product of their uncertainties is h (Planck's constant).

Hooke's Law. The stress imposed on a solid is directly proportional to the strain produced within the elastic limit.

Mendel's Principles. The Law of Segregation is that every somatic cell of an individual carries a pair of hereditary units for each character: the pairs separate during meiosis so that each gamete carries one unit only of each pair.

The Law of Independent Assortment is that the separation of units of each pair is not influenced by that of any other pair.

Murphy's Law. Anything that can go wrong will go wrong.

Ohm's Law. Electric current is directly proportional to electromotive force and inversely proportional to resistance.

Parkinson's Law. First published in *The Economist*, November 19th 1955. The author, C. Northcote Parkinson, sought to expand on the "commonplace observation that work expands so as to fill the time available for its completion". After studying Admiralty staffing levels, he concluded that in any public administrative department not actually at war the staff increase may be expected to follow this formula:

$$x = \frac{2k^m + p}{n}$$

Where k is the number of staff seeking promotion through the appointment of subordinates; p represents the difference between the ages of appointment and retirement; m is the number of hours devoted to answering minutes within the department; and n is the number of effective units being administered. Then x will be the number of new staff required each year.

Mathematicians will, of course, realise that to find the percentage increase they must multiply x by 100 and divide by the total of the previous year, thus:

$$\frac{100\,(2k^m + p)}{yn}\ \%$$

where y represents the total original staff. And this figure will invariably prove to be between 5.17% and 6.56%, irrespective of any variation in the amount of work (if any) to be done.

The Peter Principle. All members of a hierarchy rise to their own level of incompetence.

Say's Law of Markets. A supply of goods generates a demand for the goods.

Laws of Thermodynamics
1. The change in the internal energy of a system equals the sum of the heat added to the system and the work done on it.
2. Heat cannot be transferred from a colder to a hotter body within a system without net changes occurring in other bodies in the system.
3. It is impossible to reduce the temperature of a system to absolute zero in a finite number of steps.

Utz's Laws of Computer Programming. Any given program, when running, is obsolete. If a program is useful, it will have to be changed. Any given program will expand to fill all available memory.

Wolfe's Law of Journalism. You cannot hope/to bribe or twist,/ thank God! the/British journalist./But seeing what/the man will do/ unbribed, there's/no occasion to.

M

Measures

Conversions. For British, American and metric (SI) measures. Metric units not generally recommended as SI units or for use with SI are marked with an asterisk (eg Calorie*).

Acceleration

Standard gravity	=	10 metres per second squared
	=	32 feet per second squared

Area

1 square inch	=	6½ square centimetres
2 square inches	=	13 square centimetres
10¾ square feet	=	1 square metre
43 square feet	=	4 square metres
6 square yards	=	5 square metres
2½ acres	=	1 hectare
5 acres	=	2 hectares
250 acres	=	1 square kilometre
3 square miles	=	8 square kilometres

Density and concentration

4 ounces per UK gallon	=	25 grams per litre
2 ounces per US gallon	=	15 grams per litre
1 pound per cubic foot	=	16 kilograms per cubic metre
62½ pounds per cubic foot	=	1 kilogram per litre
	=	density of 1

Energy

18 British thermal units	=	19 kilojoules
4 British thermal units	=	1 kilocalorie*
1 kilocalorie* ("Calorie"*)	=	4 kilojoules

Force

7¼ poundals	=	1 newton
1 pound-force	=	4½ newtons
1 pounds-force	=	40 newtons
1 kilogram-force	=	10 newtons

Fuel consumption

5 UK gallons per mile	=	14 litres per kilometre
20 miles per UK gallon	=	7 kilometres per litre
20 miles per UK gallon	=	14 litres per 100 kilometres
5 miles per US gallon	=	6 miles per UK gallon

Length

Width of thumb	=	1 inch
	=	25 millimetres
1 inch	=	$2^1/_2$ centimetres
2 inches	=	5 centimetres
1 foot	=	30 centimetres
	=	0.3 metre
$3^1/_4$ feet	=	1 metre
39 inches	=	1 metre
11 yards	=	10 metres
$^5/_8$ mile	=	1 kilometre
5 miles	=	8 kilometres
8 miles	=	7 nautical miles (international)

Power

4 UK horsepower	=	3 kilowatts
72 UK horsepower	=	73 metric horsepower*

Pressure and stress

1 pound-force per square foot	=	48 pascals (newtons per square metre)
1 pound-force per square inch	=	7 kilopascals (kilonewtons per square metre)
1 bar	=	1 standard atmosphere
	=	$14^1/_2$ pounds-force per square inch
100 pounds-force per square inch	=	7 kilograms-force per square centimetre

Velocity (speed)

2 miles per hour	=	3 feet per second
9 miles per hour	=	4 metres per second
8 kilometres per hour	=	5 metres per second
11 kilometres per hour	=	10 feet per second
30 miles per hour	=	48 kilometres per hour
50 miles per hour	=	80 kilometres per hour
70 miles per hour	=	113 kilometres per hour

Volume and capacity

1 teaspoonful	=	5 millilitres
1 UK fluid ounce	=	28 millilitres
26 UK fluid ounces	=	25 US liquid ounces
3 cubic inches	=	49 cubic centimetres
	=	49 millilitres
$1^3/_4$ UK pints	=	1 litre
7 UK pints	=	4 litres
7 UK quarts	=	8 litres
5 UK pints	=	6 US liquid pints

9 US liquid pints	=	9 litres
1 UK gallon	=	4½ litres
2 UK gallons	=	9 litres
5 UK gallons	=	6 US gallons
1 US gallon	=	3¾ litres
4 US gallons	=	15 litres
3 cubic feet	=	85 cubic decimetres
	=	85 litres
35 cubic feet	=	1 cubic metre
4 cubic yards	=	3 cubic metres
31 UK bushels	=	32 US bushels
27½ UK bushels	=	1 cubic metre
28⅓ US bushels	=	1 cubic metre
11 UK bushels	=	4 hectolitres
14 US bushels	=	5 hectolitres
1 US bushel (heaped)	=	1¼ US bushels (struck)
1 US dry barrel	=	3¼ US bushels
1 US cranberry barrel	=	2¾ bushels
1 barrel (petroleum)	=	42 US gallons
	=	35 UK gallons
1 barrel per day	=	50 tonnes per year

Weight

1 grain	=	65 milligrams
15 grains	=	1 gram
11 ounces	=	10 ounces troy
1 ounce	=	28 grams
1 ounce troy	=	31 grams
1 pound	=	454 grams
35 ounces	=	1 kilogram
2¼ pounds	=	1 kilogram
11 stones	=	70 kilograms
11 US hundredweights	=	5 quintals*
2 UK hundredweights	=	1 quintal*
2,205 pounds	=	1 tonne
11 US tons	=	10 tonnes
62 UK tons	=	63 tonnes
100 UK (long) tons	=	112 US (short) tons

Yield

3 UK or US bushels per acre	=	2 quintals* per hectare
10 UK or US bushels per acre	=	9 hectolitres per hectare
1 UK hundredweight per acre	=	1¼ quintals* per hectare
1 UK ton per acre	=	2½ tonnes per hectare
9 pounds per acre	=	10 kilograms per hectare

Gold

The purity of gold is expressed as parts of 1,000, so that a fineness of 800 is 80% gold. Pure gold is defined as 24 carats (1,000 fine). Dental gold is usually 16 or 20 carat; gold in jewellery 9-22 carat. A golden sovereign is 22 carat.

1 metric carat = 200 milligrams

Gold and silver are usually measured in troy weights. A standard international bar of gold is 400 troy ounces; bars of 250 troy ounces are also used.

METRIC SYSTEM PREFIXES.

Prefix name & symbol		*Factor by which unit is multiplied*		*Description*
atto	a	10^{-18} =	0.000 000 000 000 000 001	
femto	f	10^{-15} =	0.000 000 000 000 001	
pico	p	10^{-12} =	0.000 000 000 001	million millionth; trillionth
nano	n	10^{-9} =	0.000 000 001	thousand millionth; billionth
micro	µ	10^{-6} =	0.000 001	millionth
milli	m	10^{-3} =	0.001	thousandth
centi	c	10^{-2} =	0.01	hundredth
deci	d	10^{-1} =	0.1	tenth
deca (or deka)	da[a]	10^{1} =	10	ten
hecto	h	10^{2} =	100	hundred
kilo	k	10^{3} =	1,000	thousand
myria	my	10^{4} =	10,000	ten thousand
mega	M	10^{6} =	1,000,000	million
giga	G	10^{9} =	1,000,000,000	thousand million; billion
tera	T	10^{12} =	1,000,000,000,000	million million; trillion
peta	P	10^{15} =	1,000,000,000,000,000	
exa	E	10^{18} =	1,000,000,000,000,000,000	

a Sometimes dk is used (eg in Germany).

UNITS WITH DIFFERENT EQUIVALENTS.

Barrel

UK (beer)	=	36 UK gallons
	=	164 litres
USA: dry standard	=	7,056 cubic inches
	=	116 litres
petroleum	=	42 US gallons
	=	159 litres
standard cranberry	=	5,826 cubic inches
	=	95.5 litres
various (liquid)	=	31–42 US gallons
	=	117–151 litres

Bushel

UK	=	2,219.36 cubic inches
	=	36.37 litres
Old English, Winchester USA[a] (struck[b])	=	2,150 42 cubic inches
	=	35.24 litres
USA (heaped[c])	=	2,747 715 cubic inches
	=	45.03 litres

a The most usual unit.
b Levelled off at the top.
c Used for apples.

Centner or Zentner

UK	=	cental of 100 pounds
	=	45.36 kilograms
Commercial hundredweight in several European countries, generally 50 kilograms	=	110.23 pounds
Metric centner of 100 kilograms	=	220.46 pounds

Chain

UK: Gunter's/surveyors'	=	66 feet
	=	20.12 metres}
Engineers'	=	100 feet
	=	30.48 metres

Foot

UK USA customary	=	12 inches
	=	0.304 8 metre

USA survey	=	12.000 02 inches
	=	0.304 800 6 metre
Canada: Paris foot	=	12.789 inches
	=	0.325 metre
Cape foot	=	12.396 inches
	=	0.315 metre

Chinese foot (*che* or *chih*):

old system	=	14.1 inches
	=	0.358 metre
new system	=	13.123 inches
	=	0.333 33 metre

Gallon

UK	=	277.42 cubic inches
	=	4.546 litres
Old English, Winchester, Wine, USA, liquid	=	231 cubic inches
	=	3.785 litres
USA, dry	=	268.802 5 cubic inches
	=	0.004 4 cubic metre

Gill

UK	=	8.669 cubic inches
	=	142.1 millilitres
USA	=	7.218 75 cubic inches
	=	118.3 millilitres

Hundredweight

UK, USA, long	=	112 pounds
	=	50.8 kilograms
USA, short	=	100 pounds
	=	45.4 kilograms

Link

UK: Gunter's/surveyors'	=	0.66 foot
	=	0.201 2 metre
Engineers'	=	1 foot
	=	0.304 8 metre

Mile

UK: imperial	=	5,280 feet
	=	1.609 344 kilometres
geographical, nautical, sea	=	6,080 feet
	=	1.853 184 kilometres[a]

a In practice 6,000 feet = 1.828 8 kilometres.

USA	=	5,280 feet
	=	1.609 344 kilometres
International nautical	=	1,852 metres
	=	6,076.12 feet

Ounce

Dry: ounce	=	437½ grains
	=	28.35 grams
ounce troy	=	480 grains
	=	31.01 grams
Liquid[a] or fluid[b] ounce: UK	=	1.734 cubic inches
	=	28.4 millilitres
USA	=	1.805 cubic inches
	=	29.6 millilitres

a 16 liquid ounces = 1 liquid pint

b 20 fluid ounces = 1 pint

Peck

UK	=	554.839 cubic inches
	=	9.092 cubic decimetres (litres)
USA	=	537.605 cubic inches
	=	8.810 cubic decimetres (litres)

Pint

UK	=	34.677 4 cubic inches
	=	0.568 litre
USA: dry	=	33.600 312 5 cubic inches
	=	0.551 cubic decimetre (litre)
liquid	=	28.875 cubic inches
	=	0.473 litre

Pound

UK } USA } avoirdupois pound	=	0.454 kilogram
USA: troy pound	=	0.373 kilogram
	=	0.823 pound (avoirdupois)
Spanish (libra)	=	0.460 kilogram
	=	1.014 pounds (avoirdupois)
"Amsterdam"	=	0.494 kilogram
	=	1.089 pounds (avoirdupois)
Danish (pund)	=	0.5 kilogram
	=	1.102 pounds (avoirdupois)
Française (livre)	=	0.490 kilogram
	=	1.079 pounds (avoirdupois)

Quart

UK	=	69.355 cubic inches
	=	1.137 litres
USA: dry	=	67.200 625 cubic inches
	=	1.101 cubic decimetres (litres)
liquid	=	57.75 cubic inches
	=	0.946 litre

Quarter

UK: capacity	=	8 bushels
	=	64 gallons
	=	2.909 hectolitres
	=	0.290 9 cubic metre
weight (mass)	=	28 pounds
	=	12.701 kilograms
cloth	=	9 inches
	=	22.86 centimetres
wines and spirits	=	27½–30 gallons
	=	125–136 litres

Quintal

Hundredweight: UK	=	112 pounds
	=	50.8 kilograms
USA	=	100 pounds
	=	45.4 kilograms
Metric quintal	=	100 kilograms
	=	220.46 pounds
Spanish quintal	=	46 kilograms
	=	101.4 pounds

Stone

UK: Imperial	=	14 pounds
	=	6.350 kilograms
Smithfield	=	8 pounds
	=	3.629 kilograms

Ton

UK: weight (mass)	=	2,240 pounds
	=	1.016 tonnes
shipping: register	=	100 cubic feet
	=	2.832 cubic metres

USA: short	=	2,000 pounds
	=	0.907 tonne
long	=	2,240 pounds
	=	1.016 tonnes
Metric ton (tonne)	=	1,000 kilograms
	=	2,204.62 pounds
Spanish: short (corta)	=	2,000 libras
	=	0.920 2 tonne
	=	2,028.7 pounds
long (larga)	=	2,240 libras
	=	1.030 6 tonnes
	=	2,272.1 pounds

See also MEASUREMENTS, page 43.

N

NATIONAL ACCOUNTS.

These are the definitions adopted by the United Nations in 1968 but national accounts now refer to gross national product as gross national income (GNI).

Final expenditure

= private final consumption expenditure ("consumers' expenditure")
+ government final consumption expenditure
+ increase in stocks
+ gross fixed capital formation
+ exports of goods and services

Gross domestic product (GDP) at market prices

= final expenditure
− imports of goods and services

Gross national income or product (GNI/GNP) at market prices

= gross domestic product at market prices
+ net property income from other countries

Gross domestic product at factor cost

= gross domestic product at market prices
− indirect taxes
+ subsidies

O

Olympic games.

I	Athens	1896	XV	Helsinki	1952
II	Paris	1900	XVI	Melbourne	1956
III	St Louis	1904	XVII	Rome	1960
IV	London	1908	XVIII	Tokyo	1964
V	Stockholm	1912	XIX	Mexico City	1968
VI	Berlin (cancelled)	1916	XX	Munich	1972
VII	Antwerp	1920	XXI	Montreal	1976
VIII	Paris	1924	XXII	Moscow	1980
IX	Amsterdam	1928	XXIII	Los Angeles	1984
X	Los Angeles	1932	XXIV	Seoul	1988
XI	Berlin	1936	XXV	Barcelona	1992
XII	Tokyo/Helsinki (cancelled)	1940	XXVI	Atlanta	1996
			XXVII	Sydney	2000
XIII	London (cancelled)	1944	XXVIII	Athens	2004
XIV	London	1948	XXIX	Beijing	2008

Organisations

These are the exact names and abbreviated titles of the main international organisations. Where membership is small or exclusive, members are listed too.

Andean community of nations. Founded in 1969.

Members

Bolivia
Colombia
Ecuador
Peru
Venezuela

Apec. Asia-Pacific Economic Cooperation. Founded in 1989, based in Singapore.

Members

Australia
Brunei
Canada
Chile
China
Hong Kong SAR
Indonesia
Japan
Malaysia
Mexico
New Zealand
Papua New Guinea
Peru
Philippines
Russia
Singapore
South Korea
Taiwan
Thailand
United States
Vietnam

ASEAN. Association of South-east Asian Nations. Established 1967.

Members

Brunei
Cambodia
Indonesia
Laos
Malaysia
Myanmar
Papua New Guinea
Philippines
Singapore
Thailand
Vietnam

BIS. Bank for International Settlements. The central bankers' central bank, in Basel. Founded 1930.

Members[a]

Australia
Austria
Belgium
Bosnia & Hercegovina
Brazil
Bulgaria
Canada
China
Croatia
Czech Republic
Denmark
Estonia
Finland
France
Germany
Greece
Hong Kong
Hungary
Iceland
India
Ireland
Italy
Japan
Latvia
Lithuania
Macedonia
Malaysia
Mexico
Netherlands
Norway
Poland
Portugal
Romania
Russia
Saudi Arabia
Singapore
Slovakia
Slovenia[a]
South Africa
South Korea
Spain
Sweden
Switzerland
Thailand
Turkey
United Kingdom
United States

a The European Central Bank is a shareholder.

CARICOM. Caribbean Community and Common Market. Formed 1973.

Members

Anguilla[a]
Antigua and Barbuda
Bahamas[b]
Barbados
Belize
British Virgin Islands[a]
Dominica
Grenada
Guyana
Haiti[c]

Jamaica
Montserrat
St Kitts-Nevis
St Lucia
St Vincent and the Grenadines
Suriname
Trinidad and Tobago
Turks and Caicos Islands[a]

a Associate member.

b Member of the Community but not the Common Market. c Not yet ratified.

Observer status
Aruba
Bermuda
Cayman Islands
Colombia
Dominican Republic
Mexico
Netherlands Antilles
Puerto Rico
Venezuela

Comesa. Common Market for Eastern and Southern Africa. Founded in 1993, with headquarters in Lusaka.

Members
Angola
Burundi
Comoros
Congo, Democratic Republic of
Djibouti
Egypt
Eritrea
Ethiopia
Kenya
Madagascar
Malawi
Mauritius
Namibia
Rwanda
Seychelles
Sudan
Swaziland
Uganda
Zambia
Zimbabwe

Commonwealth. Based in London.

Members
Antigua and Barbuda
Australia
Bahamas
Bangladesh
Barbados
Belize
Botswana
Brunei
Cameroon
Canada
Cyprus
Dominica
Fiji
The Gambia
Ghana
Grenada
Guyana
India
Jamaica
Kenya
Kiribati
Lesotho
Malawi
Malaysia
Maldives
Malta

Mauritius
Mozambique
Namibia
Nauru
New Zealand
Nigeria[a]
Pakistan[b]
Papua New gGuinea
St Kitts-Nevis
St Lucia
St Vincent and the Grenadines
Samoa
Seychelles
Sierra Leone
Singapore
Solomon Islands
South Africa[c]
Sri Lanka
Swaziland
Tanzania
Tonga
Trinidad and Tobago
Tuvalu
Uganda
United Kingdom
Vanuatu
Zambia
Zimbabwe[d]

a Membership suspended in November 1995, but renewed in May 1999.
b Pakistan was suspended in late 1999. c South Africa withdrew in 1961, but rejoined in 1994. d Suspended for one year from March 2002.

Dependencies and associated states

Australia:
Ashmore and Cartier Islands
Australian Antarctic Territory
Christmas Island
Cocos (Keeling) Islands
Coral Sea Islands Territory
Heard and McDonald Islands
Norfolk Island

New Zealand:
Cook Islands
Niue
Ross Dependency
Tokelau

United Kingdom:
Anguilla
Bermuda
British Antarctic Territory
British Indian Ocean Territory
British Virgin Islands
Cayman Islands
Channel Islands
Falkland Islands
Gibraltar
Isle of Man
Montserrat
Pitcairn Islands
South Georgia and South Sandwich Islands
St Helena – Ascension, Tristan da Cunha
Turks and Caicos Islands

COMMONWEALTH OF INDEPENDENT STATES (CIS). Founded in December 1991 by the former Soviet Socialist Republics.

Members
Armenia
Azerbaijan
Belarus
Georgia
Kazakhstan
Kirgizstan

Moldova	Tajikistan	Ukraine
Russia	Turkmenistan	Uzbekistan

ECOWAS. Economic Community of West African States. Founded 1975.

Members

Benin	Ghana	Niger
Burkina Faso	Guinea	Nigeria
Cape Verde	Guinea-Bissau	Senegal
Côte d'Ivoire	Liberia	Sierra Leone
The Gambia	Mali	Togo

EEA. European Economic Area, negotiated in 1992 between the European Community and members of EFTA, came into force in 1994 and has been maintained because the three signatories – Iceland, Norway and Liechtenstein – wanted to participate in the Single Market without being full members of the EU.

EFTA. European Free Trade Association. Established 1960.

Members

Iceland	Norway
Liechtenstein	Switzerland

EU. European Union, the collective designation of three organisations with common membership. These organisations are: the European Coal and Steel Community (ECSC), European Economic Community (EEC) and European Atomic Energy Community (EURATOM). They merged to become the European Community (EC) in 1967. In November 1993 when the Maastricht treaty came into force the EC was incorporated into the EU. EMU, Economic and Monetary Union, formed one of the articles of the Maastricht treaty, in which were set out the stages by which the EU would progress to full convergence, with a single currency, the euro.

Members

Austria	Germany[a]	Netherlands[a]
Belgium[a]	Greece	Portugal
Denmark	Ireland	Spain
Finland	Italy[a]	Sweden
France[a]	Luxembourg[a]	United Kingdom

a Founding member.

FRANC ZONE. Comité Monétaire de la Zone Franc.

Members

Benin[a]	Burkina Faso[a]	Cameroon[b]

Central African Republic[b]	Côte d'Ivoire[a]	Mali[a]
Chad[b]	Equatorial Guinea[b]	Niger[a]
Comoros[b]	French Overseas Territories[c]	Senegal[a]
Congo, Democratic Republic of[b]	Gabon[b]	Togo[a]
	Guinea-Bissau[a]	

a Member of Banque Centrale des Etats de l'Afrique de l'Ouest.

b Member of Banque des Etats de l'Afrique Centrale.

c New Caledonia, French Polynesia and the Wallis and Futuna Islands.

FTAA. Free Trade Area of the Americas. Set up in November 2002 in order to integrate the economies of the western hemisphere into a single free trade agreement. 34 members.

GCC. Co-operation Council for the Arab States of the Gulf. Its usual shorthand name is Gulf Co-operation Council. Established in 1981.

Members

Bahrain	Qatar
Kuwait	Saudi Arabia
Oman	United Arab Emirates

G7, G8, G10, G22, G26. In 1975, six countries, the world's leading capitalist countries, ranked by GDP, were represented in France at the first annual summit meeting: the United States, the UK, Germany, Japan and Italy, as well as the host country. The following year they were joined by Canada and, in 1977, by representatives of the European Union, although the group continued to be known as the G7. At the 1989 summit, 15 developing countries were also represented, although this did not give birth to the G22, which was not set up until 1998 and swiftly grew into G26. At the 1991 G7 summit, a meeting was held with the Soviet Union, a practice that continued (with Russia) in later years. In 1998, although it was not one of the world's eight richest countries, Russia became a full member of the G8. Meetings of the IMF are attended by the G10, which includes 11 countries: the original members of the G7 as well as representatives of Switzerland, Belgium, Sweden and the Netherlands.

IATA. International Air Transport Association. Head offices: Montreal, Geneva and Singapore. *Members*: most international airlines.

INTERNATIONAL SEABED AUTHORITY. An autonomous organisation in relationship with the UN. Established 1996. Based in Kingston, Jamaica. 138 member states signatory to the Convention on the Law of the Sea.

LAIA (ALADI). Latin American Integration Association. Founded in 1980, based in Montevideo.

Members[a]

Argentina	Colombia	Paraguay
Bolivia	Cuba	Peru
Brazil	Ecuador	Uruguay
Chile	Mexico	Venezuela

a There are also 14 observer countries and nine observer organisations.

b Subject to receipt of instrument of ratification.

MERCOSUR. Southern Common Market. Based in Montevideo. Founded in 1991.

Members	*Associate members*
Argentina	Bolivia
Brazil	Chile
Paraguay	
Uruguay	

NATO. North Atlantic Treaty Organisation.

Members

Belgium	Hungary	Poland
Canada	Iceland	Portugal
Czech Republic	Italy	Spain
Denmark	Luxembourg	Turkey
France[a]	Netherlands	United Kingdom
Germany	Norway	United States
Greece		

a France withdrew from the integrated military command structure.

OAU. Organization of African Unity. Known as the African Union from July 2002. Founded in 1962.

Members

Algeria	Comoros	The Gambia
Angola	Congo (Brazzaville)	Ghana
Benin	Congo, Democratic Republic of	Guinea
Botswana	Côte d'Ivoire	Guinea-Bissau
Burkina Faso	Djibouti	Kenya
Burundi	Egypt	Lesotho
Cameroon	Equatorial Guinea	Liberia
Cape Verde	Eritrea	Libya
Central African Republic	Ethiopia	Madagascar
		Malawi
Chad	Gabon	Mali

Mauritania
Mauritius
Mozambique
Namibia
Niger
Nigeria
Rwanda
São Tomé and Principe
Senegal
Seychelles
Sierra Leone
Somalia
South Africa
Sudan
Swaziland
Tanzania
Togo
Tunisia
Uganda
Western Sahara
Zambia
Zimbabwe

OAS. Organization of American States, formed in 1948. Has many permanent non-member observers.

Members

Antigua and Barbuda
Argentina
Bahamas
Barbados
Belize
Bolivia
Brazil
Canada
Chile
Colombia
Costa Rica
Cuba[a]
Dominica
Dominican Republic
Ecuador
El Salvador
Grenada
Guatemala
Guyana
Haiti
Honduras
Jamaica
Mexico
Nicaragua
Panama
Paraguay
Peru
St Kitts-Nevis
St Lucia
St Vincent and the Grenadines
Suriname
Trinidad and Tobago
United States
Uruguay
Venezuela

a Suspended in 1962.

OECD. Organisation for Economic Co-operation and Development. Capitalism's club, based in Paris. Founded in 1961. The European Commission also takes part in the OECD's work.

Members

Australia
Austria
Belgium
Canada
Czech Republic
Denmark
Finland
France
Germany
Greece
Hungary
Iceland
Ireland
Italy
Japan
Luxembourg
Mexico
Netherlands
New Zealand
Norway
Poland
Portugal
Slovakia
South Korea
Spain
Sweden
Switzerland
Turkey
United Kingdom
United States

OPEC. Organization of the Petroleum Exporting Countries. Established

1960. Based in Vienna.

Members

Algeria	Kuwait	Saudi Arabia
Indonesia	Libya	United Arab Emirates
Iran	Nigeria	Venezuela
Iraq	Qatar	

OSCE. Organization for Security and Co-operation in Europe. Originally founded in 1972 as the Conference on Security and Co-operation in Europe (CSCE). 55 members, including European countries, Canada, the United States and former republics of the Soviet Union.

SADC. Southern African Development Community. Replaced the Southern African Co-ordination Conference in 1992. Based in Gaborone, Botswana. Its aim is to work for development and economic growth in the region with common systems and institutions, promoting peace and security, and achieving complementary national and regional strategies. Fourteen members.

THE UNITED NATIONS. New York.

General Assembly	Trusteeship Council
Security Council	International Court of Justice
Economic and Social Council (ECOSOC)	

Regional Commissions		*Head office*
Economic Commission for Africa	ECA	Addis Ababa
Economic Commission for Europe	ECE	Geneva
Economic Commission for Latin America and the Caribbean	ECLAC	Santiago, Chile
Economic and Social Commission for Asia and the Pacific	ESCAP	Bangkok
Economic and Social Commission for Western Asia	ESCWA	Beirut

Other United Nations bodies		
Office for Co-ordination of Humanitarian Affairs	OCHA	New York
Office for Drug Control and Crime Prevention	ODCCP	Vienna
Office of United Nations High Commissioner for Human Rights	OHCHR	Geneva
United Nations Human Settlements Programme	UN-Habitat	Nairobi

United Nations Children's Fund	UNICEF	New York
United Nations Conference on Trade and Development	UNCTAD	Geneva
United Nations Development Programme	UNDP	New York
United Nations Environment Programme	UNEP	Nairobi
United Nations High Commissioner for Refugees	UNHCR	Geneva
United Nations Peace-keeping Operations		New York
United Nations Population Fund	UNFPA	New York
United Nations Relief and Works Agency for Palestine Refugees in the Near East	UNRWA	Gaza City, Amman
United Nations Training and Research Institutes		
World Food Programme	WFP	Rome

Specialised agencies within the UN system

Food and Agriculture Organization	FAO	Rome
International Atomic Energy Agency	IAEA	Vienna
International Bank for Reconstruction and Development (World Bank)	IBRD	Washington, DC
International Civil Aviation Organization	ICAO	Montreal
International Development Association	IDA	Washington, DC
International Finance Corporation	IFC	Washington, DC
International Fund for Agricultural Development	IFAD	Rome
International Labour Organization	ILO	Geneva
International Maritime Organization	IMO	London
International Monetary Fund	IMF	Washington, DC
International Telecommunication Union	ITU	Geneva
Multilateral Investment Guarantee Agency	MIGA	Washington, DC
United Nations Educational, Scientific and Cultural Organization	UNESCO	Paris
United Nations Industrial Development Organization	UNIDO	Vienna
Universal Postal Union	UPU	Berne
World Health Organization	WHO	Geneva
World Intellectual Property Organization	WIPO	Geneva
World Meteorological Organization	WMO	Geneva

WTO. World Trade Organisation. The international organisation of the world trading system, based in Geneva. Established in 1995 as successor to the General Agreement on Tariffs and Trade (GATT). Members: 144 countries plus the European Community.

R

Roman numerals.

I	1	**XIV**	14	**CC**	200
II	2	**XV**	15	**D**	500
III	3	**XVI**	16	**DCC**	700
IV	4	**XVII**	17	**DCCXIX**	719
V	5	**XVIII**	18	**CM**	900
VI	6	**XIX**	19	**M**	1000
VII	7	**XX**	20	**MC**	1100
VIII	8	**XXI**	21	**MCX**	1110
IX	9	**XXX**	30	**MCMXCI**	1991
X	10	**XL**	40	**MM**	2000
XI	11	**L**	50	**MMX**	2010
XII	12	**XC**	90		
XIII	13	**C**	100		

S

STATES, REGIONS, PROVINCES, COUNTIES AND LOCAL AUTHORITIES

Here are the correct spellings of the main administrative subdivisions of industrialised countries. Accents should be used. See also COUNTRIES AND THEIR INHABITANTS.

AUSTRALIA (Commonwealth of Australia)[a]

States
New South Wales
Queensland
South Australia
Tasmania
Victoria
Western Australia

Territories
Australian Capital Territory
Jervis Bay Territory
Northern Territory

a Includes Cocos (Keeling) Islands.

BELGIUM (Kingdom of Belgium)

Provinces
Antwerp
Brabant (Flemish, Walloon)
East Flanders
Hainaut
Liège
Limburg
Luxembourg
Namur
West Flanders

BRAZIL (Federal Republic of Brazil)

States
Acre
Alagoas
Amapa
Amazonas
Bahia
Ceara
Espirito Santo
Goias
Maranhao
Mato Grosso
Mato Grosso do Sul
Minas Gerais
Para
Paraiba
Parana
Pernambuco
Piauí
Rio de Janeiro
Rio Grande do Norte
Rio Grande do Sul
Rondônia
Roraima
Santa Catarina
São Paulo
Sergipe
Tocantins
Distrito Federal
(Federal District, Brasília)

CANADA

Provinces

Alberta
British Columbia
Manitoba
New Brunswick
Newfoundland
Nova Scotia
Ontario
Prince Edward Island
Quebec (Québec)
Saskatchewan

Territories

Northwest Territories
Nunavut
Yukon

FRANCE (Republic of France)

Regions

Alsace
Aquitaine
Auvergne
Basse-Normandie
Brittany (Bretagne)
Burgundy (Bourgogne)
Centre
Champagne-Ardenne
Corsica (Corse)
Franche-Comté
Haute-Normandie
Ile-de-France
Languedoc-Roussillon
Limousin
Lorraine
Midi-Pyrénées
Nord-Pas-de-Calais
Pays de la Loire
Picardy (Picardie)
Poitou-Charentes
Provence-Alpes-Côte d'Azur
Rhône-Alpes

GERMANY (Federal Republic of Germany)

States (in German *Länder*)

Baden-Württemberg
Bavaria (Bayern)
Berlin[a]
Brandenburg[b]
Bremen
Hamburg
Hesse (Hessen)
Lower Saxony (Niedersachsen)
Mecklenburg-West Pomerania (Vorpommern)[b]
North Rhine-Westphalia (Nordrhein-Westfalen)
Rhineland-Palatinate (Rheinland-Pfalz)
Saarland
Saxony (Sachsen)[b]
Saxony-Anhalt (Sachsen-Anhalt)[b]
Schleswig-Holstein
Thuringia (Thüringen)[b]

a Formerly West Berlin.

b Former East German states.

IRELAND (Republic of Ireland)

Provinces	*Counties*	
Connaught	Galway	Roscommon
	Leitrim	Sligo
	Mayo	
Leinster	Carlow	Meath
	Dublin	King's County/Offaly
	Kildare	Queen's County/ Laois
	Kilkenny	South Dublin
	King's County	Westmeath
	Longford	Wexford
	Louth	Wicklow
Munster	Clare	Limerick
	Cork	Tipperary
	Kerry	Waterford
Ulster	Cavan	Monaghan
	Donegal	

ITALY (Italian Republic)

Regions

Abruzzo
Basilicata
Calabria
Campania
Emilia-Romagna
Friuli-Venezia Giulia
Lazio
Liguria
Lombardy (Lombardia)
Marches (Marche)
Molise
Piedmont (Piemonte)
Apulia (Puglia)
Sardinia (Sardegna)
Sicily (Sicilia)
Tuscany (Toscana)
Trentino-Alto Adige
Umbria
Valle d'Aosta
Veneto

NETHERLANDS (Kingdom of the Netherlands)

Provinces

Drenthe
Flevoland
Friesland
Gelderland
Groningen
Limburg
Noord-Brabant
Noord-Holland
Overijssel
Utrecht
Zeeland
Zuid-Holland

Russia (Russian Federation)

There are 89 members (federal territorial units) of the Russian Federation. Since 1993 these members consist of 21 republics, six *krais* (provinces), 49 *oblasts* (regions), two cities of federal status (Moscow and St Petersburg), one autonomous *oblast* (the Jewish Autonomous Area) and ten *okrugs* (districts), under the jurisdiction of the *oblast* or *krai* within which they are situated. Each unit is grouped into one of seven federal districts.

Federal districts

Central
Far East
North-West
Siberian
South
Urals
Volga

Republics

Adygeya
Bashkortostan
Buryatiya
Chechnya[a]
Chuvashiya
Dagestan
Gorno-Altai
Ingushetiya
Kabardino-Balkariya
Kalmykiya
Karachayevo-Cherkessiya
Kareliya
Khakasiya
Komi
Marii-El
Mordoviya
North Osetiya-Alaniya
Sakha (Yakutiya)
Tatarstan
Tyva
Udmurtiya

a Governed federally

Krais

Altai
Khabarovsk
Krasnodar
Krasnoyarsk
Primorskii
Stavropol

Autonomous okrugs

Agin-Buryat
Chukotka
Evenk
Khanty-Mansi
Komi-Permyak
Koryak
Nenets
Taimyr
Ust-Orda Buryat
Yamal-Nenets

Spain

Autonomous Communities

Andalusia
Aragón
Asturias
Balearic Islands (Baleares)
Basque Country (Euskadi)
Canary Islands (Canarias)
Cantabria
Castilla-La Mancha
Castilla y León
Catalonia (Cataluña)
Ceuta

Extremadura
Galicia
Madrid
Melilla
Murcia
Navarra
Rioja, La
Valencian Community

UNITED KINGDOM

***England:** Unitary Authorities*

Barnsley
Bath and North-east Somerset
Birmingham
Blackburn with Darwen
Blackpool
Bolton
Bournemouth
Bracknell Forest
Bradford
Brighton and Hove
Bristol
Bury
Calderdale
Coventry
Darlington
Derby
Doncaster
Dudley
East Riding of Yorkshire
Gateshead
Halton
Hartlepool
Herefordshire
Isle of Wight
Kingston upon Hull
Kirklees
Knowsley
Leeds
Leicester
Liverpool
Luton
Manchester
Medway
Middlesborough
Milton Keynes
Newcastle upon Tyne
North-east Lincolnshire
North Lincolnshire
North Somerset
North Tyneside
Nottingham
Oldham
Peterborough
Plymouth
Poole
Portsmouth
Reading
Redcar and Cleveland
Rochdale
Rotherham
Rutland
St Helens
Salford
Sandwell
Sefton
Sheffield
Slough
Solihull
South Gloucestershire
Southampton
Southend
South Tyneside
Stockport
Stockton-on-Tees
Stoke-on-Trent
Sunderland
Swindon
Tameside
Telford and Wrekin
Thurrock
Torbay
Trafford
Wakefield
Walsall
Warrington
West Berkshire
Wigan
Windsor and Maidenhead
Wirral
Wokingham
Wolverhampton
York

***England:** Non-Metropolitan Counties*

Bedfordshire
Buckinghamshire
Cambridgeshire
Cheshire
Cornwall/Isles of Scilly
Cumbria
Derbyshire
Devon
Dorset
Durham
East Sussex
Essex
Gloucestershire
Hampshire
Hertfordshire

Isle of Wight
Kent
Lancashire
Leicestershire
Lincolnshire
Norfolk
Northamptonshire
Northumberland
North Yorkshire
Nottinghamshire
Oxfordshire
Shropshire
Somerset
Staffordshire
Suffolk
Surrey
Warwickshire
West Sussex
Wiltshire
Worcestershire

Wales: *Unitary Authorities*

Blaenau Gwent
Bridgend
Caerphilly
Cardiff
Carmarthenshire
Ceredigion
Conwy
Denbighshire
Flintshire
Gwynedd
Isle of Anglesey
Merthyr Tydfil
Monmouthshire
Neath Port Talbot
Newport
Pembrokeshire
Powys
Rhondda, Cynon, Taff
Swansea
Torfaen
Vale of Glamorgan
Wrexham

Scotland: *Unitary Authorities*

Aberdeen City
Aberdeenshire
Angus
Argyll and Bute
Clackmannanshire
Dumfries and Galloway
Dundee City
East Ayrshire
East Dunbartonshire
East Lothian
East Renfrewshire
Edinburgh, City of
Eilean Siar/Western Isles
Falkirk
Fife
Glasgow City
Highland
Inverclyde
Midlothian
Moray
North Ayrshire
North Lanarkshire
Orkney Islands
Perth and Kinross
Renfrewshire
Scottish Borders
Shetland Islands
South Ayrshire
South Lanarkshire
Stirling
West Dunbartonshire
West Lothian

Northern Ireland: *Councils*

Antrim
Ards
Armagh
Ballymena
Ballymoney
Banbridge
Belfast
Carrickfergus
Castlereagh
Coleraine
Cookstown
Craigavon
Down
Dungannon
Fermanagh
Larne
Limavady
Lisburn
Londonderry/Derry
Magherafelt
Moyle
Newry and Mourne
Newtownabbey
North Down
Omagh
Strabane

Northern Ireland: Counties

Antrim
Armagh
Belfast City
Down
Fermanagh
Londonderry/Derry
Londonderry City
Tyrone

UNITED STATES

States

Alabama (AL)
Alaska (AK)
Arizona (AZ)
Arkansas (AR)
California (CA)
Colorado (CO)
Connecticut (CT)
Delaware (DE)
Federal District of Columbia (DC)[a]
Florida (FL)
Georgia (GA)
Hawaii (HI)
Idaho (ID)
Illinois (IL)
Indiana (IN)
Iowa (IA)
Kansas (KS)
Kentucky (KY)
Louisiana (LA)
Maine (MA)
Maryland (MD)
Massachusetts (MA)
Michigan (MI)
Minnesota (MN)
Mississippi (MS)
Missouri (MO)
Montana (MT)
Nebraska (NE)
Nevada (NV)
New Hampshire (NH)
New Jersey (NJ)
New Mexico (NM)
New York (NY)
North Carolina (NC)
North Dakota (ND)
Ohio (OH)
Oklahoma (OK)
Oregon (OR)
Pennsylvania (PA)
Puerto Rico (PR)
Rhode Island (RI)
South Carolina (SC)
South Dakota (SD)
Tennessee (TN)
Texas (TX)
Utah (UT)
Vermont (VT)
Virginia (VA)
Washington (WA)
West Virginia (WV)
Wisconsin (WI)
Wyoming (WY)

a DC is not a state.

Stockmarket indices

The following is a list of major world stockmarket indices.

AUSTRALIA

S&P All Ordinaries
S&P/ASX 200
S&P/ASX 200 Res

BRAZIL

Bovespa

CANADA

S&P/TSX Metal & Mining
S&P/TSX Comp
S&P/TSX 60

FRANCE

SBF 250
MIDCAC
CAC 40

Germany
FAZ Aktien
NEMAX 50
XETRA Dax

Hong Kong
Hang Seng
HSCC Red Chip

Italy
Banca Com Ital
Mibtel General

Japan
Nikkei 225
S&P Topix 50
Topix
2nd Section

Netherlands
AEX
CBS All Share

New Zealand
Cap. 40

Russia
RTS

Singapore
SES All-Singapore
Straits Times

South Africa
FTSE/JSE All Share
FTSE/JSE Res 20
FTSE/JSE Top 40

South Korea
KOSPI
KOSPI 200

Spain
Madrid SE
IBEX 35

Sweden
OMX Index
Stockholm All-Share

Switzerland
SMI Index
SPI General

UK
FTSE100
FT30
FTSE250
FTSE All-Share

United States
DJ Industrials
DJ Composite
DJ Transport
DJ Utilities
S&P500
NASDAQ Cmp
NASDAQ 100
Russell 2000
NYSE Comp.
Willshire 5000

Cross-border indices
DJ Stoxx 50
DJ Euro Stoxx 50
DJ Global Titans 50
Euronext 100
Next 150
FTSE Multinatls
FTSE Global 100
FTSE4Good Global
FTSE E300
FTSE E100
FTSE Latibex
MSCI World$

CROSS-BORDER INDICES cont.
MSCI ACWI Free
MSCI Europe
MSCI EMU
MSCI Pacific
S&P Global 1200
S&P Europe 350
S&P Euro

Source: *Financial Times.*

INDEX

A

abbreviations 6–7
  ampersands in 6
  business, list of 98–101
  currencies 6
  dates 7
  definite article with 6
  elements 6, 7
  formed of upper and lower case letters 6–7
  full form on first appearance 6
  international bodies 6, 141–50
  Internet 123–5
  lower case when written in full 7
  members of Parliament 7
  numerals in 6–7
  scientific units 6–7
  small capitals in 6, 7, 69
  titles of people 7
  two together 7
  units of measurement 7
  very familiar 6
  which can be pronounced 6
-able, -eable, -ible 7–8
abstract nouns, number of verb governed by 19
accents 8
  foreign 101
  on French, German, Spanish, Portuguese names and words 8
  on words accepted as English 8
accountancy terms 12, 101–2
  American and British English compared 95–6
acronyms 8
  see also abbreviations
active tense, prefer to passive 1, 8
acts of parliament, capitals for 14
address, forms of 75–7
  abbreviated 7
adjectives
  formed from two or more words, use of hyphens 35–6
  hyphenated, in AmEng 87
  use for precision 78
adverbs
  position of in AmEng and BrEng 10, 82–3
  position in BrEng 9, 10
  wrong usage 34
used adjectivally with hyphens 36
aircraft names 30, 40
ambiguities, hyphens to avoid 35
American English
  and British English accounting terminology 95–6
  and BrEng 82–96
  exclusivity, AmEng and BrEng 82
  hyphenation 87
  problem words, AmEng and BrEng 84–5, 86, 87–93
  punctuation 93–4
  spelling 69–70
Americanisms, use in BrEng 9–10; *see also* Part II
Americans, what to call them 22, 27
ampersands 10–11
  in abbreviations 6
an or a 11
animals and plants, usage for 11
antithesis, use of colon for 62
apostrophes 62
  after plurals 62
Arab names 47
areas, capitals or lower case for 15–16
article
  definite, in abbreviations 6
  definite, in names of newspapers 40
  definite, with place names 53
  indefinite 10–11, 19
astronomical unit 11

B

Bangladeshi names 47
Beaufort Scale 103–4
Bible, books of the 40
books, titles of
  punctuation 40
  italic or roman 40
brackets 62
  and position of commas 63

British English
and American English 82–96
spelling 69–74
buildings, capitals for 16

C
calendars 105–6
calibres 30
capitals 13–18
small, in abbreviations 6–7
for ranks, titles, offices 13–14
historical periods 17
miscellaneous 17; *see also* lower case
captions 76
cars, international vehicle registration letters 106–8
cedilla 8, 101
century 24
Chinese names 47
circumflex 8, 101
circumlocutions, avoid 1–2
cities
capital, avoid use as synonyms for governments 53
instances of use of lower case 16
list of largest 108–9
spelling 52
clauses
commas round inserted 62–3
hanging 34
collective nouns 18–19
number of verb governed by 18–19
colons 62
American usage 93
commas 62–3
in dates 63
in lists, AmEng compared with BrEng 93
commissions, lower case for ad fhoc 14
committees, lower case for ad hoc 14
commodities, SITC descriptions 109–12
companies, stockmarket listings 158–60
company names 19, 20, 69
ampersands in 10
compass, hyphens for quarters of 36
compass points, upper or lower case 16
conditional sentences 43
constituencies, compounds, ampersands in 10
counties
correct spellings of 152–8
countries
what to call them 21–2
countries, singular form of verb with 19
cross-references in proof-reading 57
currencies 22–3, 113–17
abbreviations 6, 23, 113–17
British, American 23
capitals for 23
list of countries and symbols 113–17
lower case or capitals 15, 23
punctuation of abbreviated form 6
ranges 23
currency, standard 23
cyber-terms 27

D
dashes 63
AmEng usage compared with BrEng 94
in dates 38
with figures 29–30
data 24
dates 7, 23, 30
"as of" in, avoid, 11
dashes in 38
hyphens in 38
punctuation of 24, 62, 63
when referring to 11, 42
decimals and fractions 29, 121
departments, capitals for 14
dictionary, AmEng and BrEng 84–5
diminutives, avoid 77
Dutch names 47–8

E
earthquakes 118

e-expressions 17, 26
elements
  capitals for 7
  isotopes of 7
  list of names and symbols 119–20
em-rule, em-dash 94
en-rule, en-dash 94
ethnic groups
  AmEng and BrEng 83
  references to 27
euphemisms, avoid 2, 27
euro- and Euro-terms 7, 16–17, 35

F
family names, *see* surnames
figures (numbers) 29–30, 52
  hyphens or dashes with 29–30
  ranges 29
figures of speech 1, 50; *see also* metaphors; similes
finance, capitals in references to 14–15
fonts, wrong 57
footnotes 40
foreign names 47–8
  capitals in 47–8
  problematical 51
foreign phrases, avoid 1
foreign titles, *see* titles of people
foreign words and phrases 31
  accents on 8
  anglicised 39–40
  italics for 8, 39–40
  prefer Eng alternative 31
Fowler, H.W. 3, 62
fractions 29, 30, 121
  decimal equivalents 121
  hyphens in 30, 34
French
  names and words, accents and cedillas 8
  names 48
full stops 63
  in abbreviations, AmEng and BrEng 94
  with initials 39

G
games, number of verb governed by 19
gender 2, 33
genitive 33
  of abbreviations 6
geographical areas, initial capitals 16
geographical assumptions, in writing 82
geographical names
  altered forms in historical references 16
  see also place names
geological eras 122
German names 48
German names and words, umlauts 8, 101
gold, measures for 134
government
  capital cities referring to 53
  initial capitals in references to 14–15
  institutions, English form 69
  singular form of verb 19
Gowers, Sir Ernest 18, 63
Gross, John 4

H
Hart's rules 63
Hazlitt, William 1
he/she 2, 67–8
headings
  no full stop at end 63
  omit titles of people 75–6
historical periods, upper case 17
historical references, altered forms of geographical names 16
hyphens 34–8
  in abbreviations 6
  no need for 35, 36–8
  avoid overuse of 38
  in dates 38
  different AmEng and BrEng conventions 87
  with figures 29–30
  in names 47
  separating identical letters 36

three-word 38
to avoid ambiguities 35
two-word 37–8
in word breaks 61
hypothesis, subjunctive in 3, 43

I

imperatives, avoid 2
imperial measures 43, 95
infinitives, split 74
initials
omit middle names 77
use of points 39
institutions, capitals for 14–15
interest-groups
assumptions about sex of 68
circumlocutions promoted by 1
Internet abbreviations 123–5
interpolations, in direct quotations 64
intransitive verbs 18
inverted commas, *see* quotation marks
Italian names 48
italics 39–40
foreign words in 8

J

Jane's "All The World's Aircraft" 30
Japanese names 48
jargon, avoid 1, 41
Johnson, Dr Samuel 21
journalese 68–9

K

Korean names 47, 48

L

Latin
names for animals, plants, etc 11
avoid 31
and italics 40
words and phrases, with translations 126–8
laws, scientific, economic, facetious and fatalistic 129–30
lawsuits, italics for *versus* or *v* 40
layout mistakes 57
local authorities, correct spellings of 152–8
lower case
in abbreviations 6–7
ad hoc organisations 14
cyber-terms 27
miscellaneous uses 16–18
for office holders 13–14
for ranks or titles not followed by names 13
for rough descriptions 14

M

Malaysian titles of people 76
"man" words, alternatives to 68
manufactured goods, SITC descriptions 109–12
marginal marks, in proof-reading 58–60
may and might 43
measurements 43
American units compared with British 95
astronomical 11
imperial 43, 95
lower case for abbreviated forms 6–7
metric 134
national preferences 43
measures
conversions 131–9
gold 134
units with different equivalents 135–9
metaphors 1, 44–6
metric units 95
list of 131–3
prefixes 134
ministries, capitals for 14

N

names 47–8
difficult spellings 51–2
capitals for proper 15
national accounts, United Nations definitions 140

nationalities
  precision in reference to 21–2
  American usage 83–4
newspapers
  definite articles in names of 40
  italics for names of 40
nicknames, avoid 77
no and yes votes 16
nouns
  ending in -s but treated as singular 19
  formed from prepositional verbs with hyphens 36
  used as verbs 10, 75, 76, 82
  see also collective nouns; proper nouns
number, use of verb with 18–19
numbers
  in abbreviations 6–7
  figures or words 29–30

O

office holders
  lower case for 13
  hyphens 35
  plurals 55
Olympic Games 141
opposition (government), lower case for 14
organisations
  when lower case 14
  capitals for 14–15
  definite article with abbreviated form 6
  list with abbreviated titles 141–50
Orwell, George 1, 3, 44

P

page references, spelling 7
Pakistani names 47
pamphlets
  punctuation of titles 40
  titles in roman 40
paragraphs, length of 3
parenthesis, dashes for 63
participles, use of 2
partnership, singular form of verb 19
passive tense, prefer active 1, 8
percentages 29, 30, 52
periodicals, italics for names of 40
periods, *see* full stops; points
personal names
  foreign, *see* foreign names
  initials 39, 77
  titles, *see* titles of people
  see also surnames
Pinyin spelling 47
place names 52–4
  changes of name 52
  definite article with 53
  English form 52
  spellings of difficult 53–4
places, initial capitals for 15–16
  lower case for 16
plays
  punctuation of titles 40
  titles 40
plurals 18–19
  in abbreviations 6
  to avoid sexism 68
  spelling of certain 54–6
  see also plurals
points, *see* full stops; initials
political area, initial capitals 16
political party
  capitals for 15
  singular form of verb 18
political terms, upper case 15–16
possessives, apostrophes in 62
prefixes 26
  with hyphens 35
  metric system 134
prepositions
  after verbs, be sparing in use of 78
  in dates 29–30, 38
  position with "both" and "and" 12;
  see also prepositions
proofreading 57–61
  marks 58–60
proper names 15
provinces, correct spellings of 152–8
punctuation 62–4

of abbreviated measurements 6–7
differences in AmEng and BrEng 87, 93–5
placing with quotation marks 62, 63–4, 94

Q

question-marks 64
quotation marks 63–4
AmEng compared with BrEng 94–5
and punctuation placing 63–4
for titles of books, pamphlets etc 40
uses of single and double 63–4
quotations
broken off and resumed 63–4
interpolations in direct 64
use of colon before 62

R

race 27
AmEng and BrEng terms 27, 83
radio programmes 40
ratios
accountancy 101–2
words or figures 29
regions
capitals or lower case for 15–16
correct spellings of 152–8
Richter scale for earthquakes 118
Roman numerals 7, 151
rough descriptions, in lower case 14
Russian names 48

S

scientific units named after individuals, abbreviations 7
scientific words, avoid 1
second names, *see* surnames
semi-colons 64
sentence structure, AmEng and BrEng 82–3
sentences
conditional 43
ending in prepositions 56
keep short 3, 63
never start with figures 29
use simple 3
sex, or gender 33
sexism 67–8
AmEng and BrEng 83–4
ships 40
short words, prefer 1, 68
SI units 95, 131–3
silver, measures for 134
similes 1
Singaporean names 47
small capitals, for abbreviations 6, 7, 69
spacecraft names, italics for 40
Spanish accents 101
special groups, ad hoc in lower case 14
spelling 69–74
different AmEng and BrEng conventions 82–3, 86, 84–93
split infinitives 74
square brackets 62
Standard International Trade Classification (SITC) 109–12
states
correct spellings of 152–8
instances of use of lower case 16
stockmarket indices 158–60
subjunctive, use of 3, 43
suffixes 7–8, 74
AmEng -ize and BrEng -ise 84
-ise 70, 84
different AmEng and BrEng conventions 86–7
surnames
and forenames 75–6
in headings or captions 76
order in foreign names 47
syntax, AmEng and BrEng 82–3

T

technical terms 41
television programmes 40
temperatures 6–7
tense, perfect 10
tilde 8, 101
times 75

titles of people 75–7
  of aristocracy 77
  capitals for 13–14
  for the dead 76
  first mention 75
  foreign 76
  hyphens in 35
  misleading 75
  women 77
trade names, upper case 17
transitive verbs 18, 24, 34, 80
translation of a foreign name, lower case for rough 14
treasury bills, bonds 15
treaties, capitals for 14
"typos" 57

U

Ukrainian names 48
umlauts 8, 101
upper case, *see* capitals

V

verbs
  with collective nouns 18–19
    prepositional 36; *see also* intransitive, transitive
Vietnamese names 47
vocabulary
  AmEng and BrEng 82
  differences between AmEng and BrEng 82ff

W

Wade-Giles system 47
wars, usage for 80
which and that 80
women
  American usage 84
  married but known by maiden names 77
  preferred titles 77
word breaks 57, 61
  hyphens in 61
words to avoid 78